Compliments of the
John A. Walker College of Business
with funding provided by:

BB&T

The Boyles Family

Duke Power Company Foundation

First Citizens Bank

North Carolina Alliance
for Community Financial Institutions

Wachovia Corporation

Keeper of the Public Purse

The Story of Public Finance in North Carolina. Phenomenal growth in taxing and spending. Modest growth in the number of people served. A coming clash between taxpayers and taxusers.

by

Harlan E. Boyles

TREASURER OF NORTH CAROLINA

with Charles Heatherly

North Carolina State Budget

1964-1994

(Budget in Billions; Population in Millions)

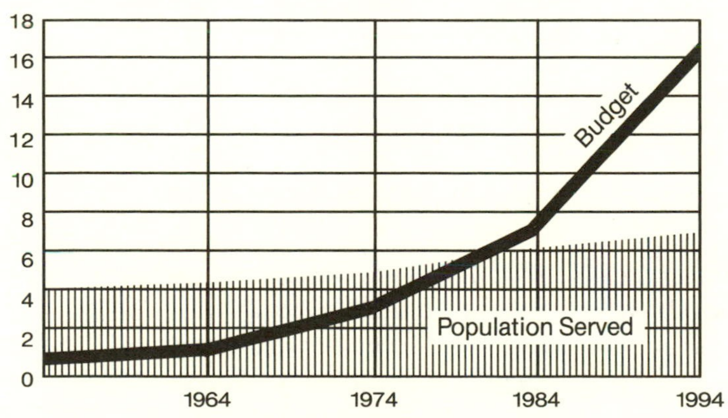

Appalachian State University
Boone, North Carolina

Proceeds from the sale of this book to go to the Harlan E. Boyles Distinguished CEO Lecture Series at the John A. Walker College of Business

Cover design by Spec & Set, Inc., Raleigh, N.C.

Printed in the United States of America.

ISBN 0-9634559-1-5

With special gratitude to friends of Appalachian State University whose financial assistance and generosity made this project possible:

Mr. Robert W. Doran
Chairman and Managing Partner
Wellington Management Company
Boston, Massachusetts

Mr. William R. Holland
Chairman and Chief Executive Officer
United Dominion Industries
Charlotte, North Carolina

Mr. G. A. Sywassink
Chairman and Chief Executive Officer
Standard Holding Corporation
Charlotte, North Carolina
and
Chair, Business Advisory Council
John A. Walker College of Business

Acknowledgements

I am deeply appreciative to a number of people who have helped research material for this book, reviewed early drafts and advised on the accuracy and relevance of a number of issues: Thomas H. Campbell and Stephen F. Albright of the Treasurer's Office for assisting with the overall project; economist Dr. Charles D. Liner, for his able advise and counsel; historians Dr. Jerry L. Cross and Dr. Jerry C. Cashion for their insight and knowledge of the historical aspects of public finance; S. Nicole Underwood and Alex F. Wallace of the N.C. Department of Revenue for their able assistance in obtaining tax data; Dr. Rick Kirkpatrick for his thoughtful insights in finalizing this manuscript; Marsha Turner for her editorial assistance; and, Deborah Culler for her clerical assistance.

A Personal Note

As hard as we have tried to avoid inconsistencies with our numbers, there may be from time to time discrepancies among the various budget figures cited. That is because of the variations in accounting and reporting practices currently applicable to the reporting of the State's budgetary receipts and expenditures. In some instances, our data came from historical documents, and in other instances, we may have had to rely on appropriation authorization documents, which change. In some instances, we were not sure whether the reported receipts were gross figures or were net of refunds and reimbursements–a fact which cannot be discerned from the current budget. In the final analysis, our numbers will vary and their consistency will depend upon the source of the documents we relied upon. This obvious deficiency and weakness in the State's accounting and reporting system is something that is in urgent need of attention and correction.

In every case, however, we have made a sincere and diligent effort to make a full and accurate accounting of North Carolina's public finance. That is the duty of the Keeper of the Public Purse.

HEB

Prologue

Public finance is an exciting and dynamic profession. Far from being the profession of dullards, as many often suggest, finance is one of the most interesting, intriguing and significant occupations. Public finance has been my life's work and I am grateful for the opportunity to have served in this noble calling.

I am humbled by the awesome challenges which face North Carolina and our nation as we approach the twilight of the 20th century and await the dawn of a new age. In this transition, which also coincides with a career that spans nearly a half century, I am proud of the job we have done in North Carolina in achieving one of the very best records in all America of managing our public finances wisely and prudently. North Carolina's fiscal record today is the envy of the entire nation. This splendid record of managing our public finance in North Carolina is a source of great pride for our people and their leaders. But more than that, it translates everyday into savings which are passed along to the taxpayers.

There is reason for concern. Our State budget has increased too rapidly in recent years. Its growth exceeds the growth of our population. It exceeds the rate of inflation. And, it exceeds our ability to manage wisely the expansion of existing programs and the addition of new programs. The growth of State government, if it continues unabated at its present rate, will soon exceed the ability of our citizens to pay their taxes. It is time we examine both the scope and role of State government in North Carolina and make the needed adjustments so that our public expenditures will serve the public purpose, as required by our constitution. Otherwise, we risk losing the confidence of our people without which the republic cannot endure.

I have shared my best advice and counsel with governors and legislators for the past four decades. Often they took it. Sometimes they did not agree. Now, I offer the best of my experience to the people of North Carolina. In your hand is the power to change things or the power to leave things as they are. By choosing those who represent you in public office, you influence public policy. Ultimately, the power of the public purse is in your hands.

Harlan E. Boyles

Taxes are what we pay for civilized society.
Justice Oliver Wendell Holmes

Contents

The power to tax involves the power to destroy.
Justice John Marshall

Tables

Figures

Appendices

Chapter 1

North Carolina Public Finance: An Overview

The value of a dollar is to buy just things: a dollar goes on increasing in value with all the genius and all the virtue of the world. A dollar in a university is worth more than a dollar in a jail; in a temperate, schooled, law-abiding community than in some sink of crime where dice, knives and arsenic are in constant play.

Ralph Waldo Emerson

In my time, I have seen America become the moral and economic leader of the world. We achieved this greatness with hard work, thrift, discipline and a sense of values based on honesty, integrity, fairness, and a respect for the rights and well-being of other people.

North Carolina grew strong and great during this period as well. We grew a vibrant farm economy and saw it diversify. We sold industry on the great potential that existed within our borders and they came, creating new jobs.

America's fortunes have changed as we now watch the clock count down the final ticks of the great 20th century. In the span of just one decade, or maybe two, we have watched with trepidation as our nation went from being the financial leader of the world to the largest debtor nation. We seemed to have lost our moral compass, as well.

But as our nation's financial fortunes have shrunk, North Carolina has risen head and shoulders above the rest of the states. North Carolina has emerged from the economic chaos which exists all around us with one of the strongest and best managed financial records of all the states. And yet, even here there are troubling signs that our leaders are tempted to turn from the traditions of hard work and thrift to the misguided policy of "spend now and worry later" that has caused so much misery elsewhere.

My own generation deserves many accolades for the advances it has brought in better medicine, communications, transportation and other trappings of high technology. The average American home today is equipped with devices of convenience, comfort and necessity that only the very, very rich enjoyed when I was a child.

My generation also deserves censure for using up more of the nation's wealth than we created and we are the first generation in American history to do that. We are leaving a national debt to our posterity which exceeds the gross domestic product. That is indefensible and will become a source of greater grief for the next generation as it begins to grapple with the problems of its time and finds that its choices are severely limited. But even worse, there is little left standing to show for what the money was spent. It was not spent for advances in education and science nor for other lasting improvements that would have made life better for future generations. Instead, the borrowed money of the 1980s and 1990s was consumed by the providers of medical care, by government workers and retirees, by investors of poorly managed savings and loan institutions and eventually by investors in the public debt.

Even at this writing, our national leaders are spending nearly $1 billion a day, which we don't have, for the same ephemeral things just noted. The disaster that awaits us is like that of the train headed for a broken bridge. Instead of stopping the train and repairing the bridge, our Congressional engineers have chosen to increase the speed, thus assuring that the calamity will be sooner and with greater destruction.

We are fortunate in North Carolina to have managed our fiscal affairs so as to avoid, at least on the State level, some of the anguish which will occur when future national leaders confront the reality that we have lived beyond our means and it is time to set things straight. North Carolinians can take pride and comfort in the fact that our budget is balanced, as required by the State constitution and that our financial footing is sound.

However, there is reason for concern in that the General Assembly in recent years has begun to imitate some of the bad habits of our national Congress and spend too much money for things that may not meet the public purpose, as required by our constitution, and for things which, arguably, will not make North Carolina a better place. It is time that we revisit our financial priorities and practices so that we do not burden our children with our own folly.

Such are the reasons why we should study public finance with considerable seriousness.

What is Public Finance?

The study of public finance is exciting and challenging because it deals with money—the fuel that runs the public engine. Public finance is the system for managing public funds, which consist of money that belongs to the people. With money and the public faith, government can do a great deal of good. Without money and without public confidence, government becomes impotent, at best; tyrannical, at worst.

The process of managing public money is not unlike the process with which a person should attempt to manage his or her own personal affairs. To live a good and happy life, a person should earn enough money to provide for current living expenses, food, shelter, clothing and reasonable amenities. In addition, a prudent person will save for future needs—education for the children, retirement, vacation travel, a larger home, and other necessities and amenities.

When I contemplated the purchase of our family's first home, it was a major decision. My young wife and I were just starting a family and the small apartment in which we lived was not adequate. Our major concern was the additional cost of buying a home. I was almost overwhelmed by the 61 percent increase in the monthly mortgage payment above what I was then paying in rent for the apartment. The idea of committing to a 25-year mortgage at what was then a burdensomely high interest rate of four and one-half percent also took courage.

We bought that home in 1956 and resolved to find a way to make the $89 monthly mortgage payment, which at that time seemed like an awful lot more money than the $55 monthly rent we were paying. That was a good decision in retrospect.

Except for the amount of money involved, and the scope of many different types of expenditures, the State's budget process is similar to that of the typical family.

Instead of earning its money, the State taxes its people to raise funds, which are called revenue. In doing so, the State assumes the responsibility of accounting for all the money it spends, called expenditures, so that all taxpayers are treated fairly.

North Carolina's constitution specifically requires that all tax expenditures be used only for "the public purpose." In the early days of our history, our leaders interpreted the public purpose quite narrowly, choosing to fund only the most essential matters—public safety, crime, education, roads and making laws. Now, we spend money for almost any and every purpose for which a special interest group can think of bringing a do-good proposition to Raleigh.

This book is a discussion of North Carolina's financial affairs over the course of two centuries. It is the story of how our people carved a civilization from the vast wilderness which greeted the first European explorers. The first settlers came to America, and to the Carolina Colony, to escape tyranny, high taxes and harsh conditions in the old country and to seek a better opportunity in the new land. They came and they built a great civilization of which we enjoy the fruits today. The challenge for us is to re-examine the way we manage our wealth today so that our children and our grandchildren can look forward to a good life, too.

Growth

The main characteristic of North Carolina's public finance over its two centuries of history has been growth–stupendous growth. The amount of money which the State of North Carolina has collected in taxes and spent on behalf of the public purpose has increased faster than the growth of its population. Its spending has grown faster than the rate of inflation. In fact, there is no comparable object, animate or inanimate, which has grown as rapidly as the public purse.

Consider these facts. Between the years 1800 and 1900 North Carolina's population grew by a factor of 4.0. Again during the next century the State's population also expanded 3.9 times.

The State budget, however, increased 20 fold between 1800 and 1900 (in 1994 dollars) and between 1900 and 2000 our budget will have increased 278 times. That is based on the assumption that the North Carolina budget grows at the same rate during the last half of the 1990s decade as it did during the first half–a conservative assumption in view of our current spending practices.

In short, while the State's population has grown steadily at about the same rate over two centuries, its taxation and spending policies have grown exponentially. These figures–projected into the next century–suggest that by the year 2100 North Carolina's population will total 26 million and that our State budget will exceed $1.5 trillion. Of course, we know that is not likely. While our beautiful State may be large enough to support a population of that magnitude, it could do so only with a severe degradation in the quality of life for all of our people.

More difficult to imagine than the population explosion is the projected rise in public spending. To support such a colossal appetite, the State would have to tax 100 percent of the income of its entire population. We know that isn't possible because that would leave no taxes for either the federal or local governments and it would leave nothing for

Table 1-1. North Carolina Budget and Population Growth, 1800-2000

	Year 1800	Year 1900	Year 2000
Population	478,000	1,900,000	7,400,000
Population Increase		4.0X	3.9X
Budget (1994$)	$4 Million	$79 Million	$22 Billion
Budget Increase		20X	278X

the people themselves to live on. Long before this happened the State would be a place of anarchy and rebellion.

This scenario, I am sad to say, is not an exaggeration. It is a true depiction of what has happened in the public finance in our State. Most of the growth has taken place in the last third of this century. North Carolina's first billion dollar State budget was adopted in 1964, and our first $2 billion budget in 1971. It had taken us 175 years to reach our first billion-dollar budget but we doubled that feat in only seven years.

As we examine North Carolina's fiscal matters, one point worth noting is that most of the State's money goes to pay its 217,000 employees and provide their medical and retirement benefits. Some 51 percent of the State budget is for payroll and employee benefits. Of the education budget, payroll and employee benefits account for 84 percent of the total.

In 1964, there were 108,000 State employees, including teachers, and the total North Carolina budget was $1.2 billion. Since that time, the budget has increased 16-fold and the number of State employees has more than doubled. During the same period of time our population increased just 50 percent.

An overwhelming portion of the budget growth has been consumed by support for our public schools and our institutions of higher education. As any prudent financial manager should do, we should ask ourselves, "Have we gotten value for our money?" This should not be a rhetorical exercise.

The fastest growing portion of the State budget in the 1990s, however, has become public assistance, particularly the State's share of the federally mandated Medicaid program which pays for medical care for the poor. The primary consequence of our publicly funded medical care programs, we should remember, is the transfer of wealth from taxpayers to the providers of medical care at very high costs. Together with what we spend for welfare and other social relief programs, North Carolina's public assistance spending is the second largest item in the budget and is nearing the total amount we spend for all education programs. If it continues to grow at its present rate, by the year 2000, North Carolina's largest budget outlay will be consumed by public assistance initiatives.

State government has grown during the past three decades faster than our population, faster than the earnings of our people and, perhaps, faster than our need for basic and essential public services. That is because our political leaders have adopted the mentality that the most common solution to most problems is "more money." This "more money" mentality always means higher costs for the taxpayers, but it does not always solve the problem.

No one argues that the quality of government services has improved by a factor of 16 during the past 30 years—a time of such great increase in public expenditures. Ample evidence to the contrary exists in the decline of our public schools, increased crime and greater concern over environmental decay during a time in which our government was spending billions to deal with these problems. The fact that funding for public assistance is the fastest growing part of our State budget should be alarming news to every taxpayer.

It is clear that after years of failed experiments bigger government does not mean better government. We must abandon this notion and instead seek to make government smarter.

Change Is Needed

I do not believe our people can endure the increased tax burden necessary to sustain the rate of growth of the trend already in place. It isn't mathematically possible. It isn't politically possible. Here are changes which I believe we must make to restore reason to our State policies and order to our way of life:

1. **Reinvent government—Make government serve the public purpose, as it is intended to do. Make government efficient, responsive and effective. Make government accountable by establishing measurable goals and providing periodic evaluation. Eliminate unneeded programs.**

2. **Reform education.**

3. **Eliminate federal mandates.**

4. **Re-focus economic development.**

5. **Make government more participatory.**

6. **Establish a balance of power between the executive and legislative branches.**

7. **Make government work to serve the people, rather than force the people to bear the burden of a bloated, lethargic bureaucracy.**

RECOMMENDATION #1

Reinvent government. Much has been made in recent years of the notion that it is time to change the priorities of our government programs and the way we provide public services. Government simply has grown too big, lethargic and unresponsive to the will and needs of the people.

Budget Reform

Our transformation of State government ought to begin with the budget. It is too large and growing almost uncontrollably. The laxity with which we adopt and manage the budget encourages inefficiency, invites wasteful expenditures and fails to address the urgent needs of our society in a timely and effective manner.

Public spending is increasing in North Carolina during the mid-1990s at the alarming rate of nearly $1 billion a year.

Emphasize Product Over Process

A basic problem with government as it functions today is the emphasis upon process and neglect of the product. It is a common misconception among many public officials that the process of being busy, the process of doing something, if nothing more than filing papers, the process of attending meetings, is enough to justify one's job. This is not so in the private sector and it should not be so in government employment.

Instead, North Carolina government employees should subscribe to, and really believe in, the State motto–*Esse Quam Videri.* It means simply, "To Be, Rather Than To Seem."

To earn his or her pay in the future, the public employee should produce a product or a quantifiable service much like the citizen who works in the private sector. The state-employed educator of the future must work intelligently so that students will learn what they should know in order to qualify for meaningful jobs that pay a decent wage.

All public employees must produce a product or a service that is worth the cost of their time, otherwise their positions ought to be eliminated. And, they should be rewarded accordingly when they do an excellent job.

We should begin our examination of government with the budget. Nothing short of a major overhaul of the budgeting process will suffice. Instead of rubber-stamping the continuation budget, both the Governor and the General Assembly should begin an exhaustive examination of every program. Instead of automatically re-funding ongoing programs with modest cost-of-living increases, the basic purpose and the effectiveness of each program should be carefully examined during each biennial budget review. The time has come to adopt a zero-based budget procedure.

Each program should be judged on its efficiency, its effectiveness and its relevance. Those programs which are needed but are no longer effective should be improved. Those programs no longer needed must be abolished to make room for ones which have greater importance.

We must take a different approach in personnel management. Promotion should be made on the basis of performance, not seniority and not political suitability.

And finally, we must get away from the notion that a State job is guaranteed for life. In this era of downsizing which has seen the retirement incentive offered by many major companies vanish, the security of government pensions becomes even more attractive. However, the government pension should be treated as an incentive for building employee morale, loyalty and high performance.

The way in which the State has come to lease office space is a good example of an area in need of better management. During the decade from 1985 through 1994, the amount of State leased office space almost doubled from 1.69 million square feet to 3.17 million square feet. The money we spend annually on leased office space tripled, during that same period, from $8 million to $26 million. The State workforce increased only 18 percent during that time, yet most of the new employees were teachers and other school and prison employees who do not require space in State office buildings. Instead of leasing so much space, the State would be wiser to apply these rather substantial lease payments to construction costs for State-owned facilities which, when amortized over the life of the property, would be a far better value for taxpayers. In doing so, the State would be getting back more than its cancelled check.

There is considerable reason to believe that our State workforce has grown too fast and that the number of State employees exceeds the essential work for them to do.

RECOMMENDATION #2

Reform education. The major work that must be done is the challenge we face in changing our public schools so that our students graduate with the knowledge they must possess to earn a decent livelihood or prepare for higher education.

Our public schools are a dismal failure by all known and measurable indicators. Student achievement is low. Student disruptions and incidents of violence in the schools are increasing.

The problem is not entirely the fault of the schools. There is considerable evidence that some of the fault lies with parents who take little interest in their children's school work. Parents play a vital role in setting the priorities of their children. It is an irrefutable, statistical fact that children of parents who value education and set such an example do better in school than students from homes where learning is not held in high esteem.

Good parents influence their children in many ways, by instilling in them a love of learning, and by teaching them discipline and respect for others.

But there are things about the way we operate our schools which need to be changed.

First, we should change the governance procedure which is a mess and which everyone agrees does not work. In North Carolina, the chief executive officer of our public schools is elected statewide. He is charged with carrying out the policy of the State Board of Education whose members are appointed by the Governor. Members of the Board too often have been chosen for their political support of the Governor, rather than their educational credentials. None of this matters much anyway because the General Assembly has, in fact, acted as the chief education policymaker for the past half century. Whatever our schools are, good or bad, the General Assembly deserves the credit, or blame, because it has made all of the major policy decisions affecting our public schools.

There are two ways to achieve better management of our public schools. Name the Superintendent of Public Instruction as Chairman of the Board of Education. Give him a vote and make him the presiding officer of the Board. The General Assembly should back off its policy of meddling with our schools and allow the Governor, the Board of Education and the Superintendent to do their jobs.

The proper role for the General Assembly is to provide funding and set performance goals. The proper role for the Board of Education is to establish and administer the policy for achieving those goals. And the proper role for the Superintendent is to carry out that policy. Under our present system, the Superintendent, the Board of Education, the Governor, and the General Assembly are all engaged in making school policy, much of it redundant and confusing.

Another option would be to abolish the elective superintendent post and make this job appointive by the Board of Education. If this change is adopted, the Board should be given broader powers to carry out the goals and policy set by the General Assembly. It is unlikely that any significant progress can be made improving North Carolina's public schools until this governance issue is addressed effectively.

Reward Performance

Here is another major reason why our public schools don't work well. Public education is the only profession where if you do a good job nothing good happens. If you do a bad job nothing bad happens. Nothing important happens, regardless whether school employees do a good job or a bad job because that is the law. Employees are rewarded for how long they stay on the job rather than for what kind of job they do. It should come as no surprise then, in the absence of incentives either to do good or avoid doing bad things, school employees will not excel. Our public school law in North Carolina, as in many other states, mandates mediocrity. In the absence of setting excellence as a goal, the law establishes minimum standards of performance. In doing so, the minimum which the law requires becomes the maximum that can be required.

At the heart of this issue is the Fair Employees Dismissal Act, also called the teacher's tenure law, which makes it very difficult to fire or discipline a teacher in North Carolina for anything short of a major criminal offense. If the teacher is entitled to any special protection, real or perceived, the disciplinary process is rigged so much in favor of the teacher that school administrators are reluctant to take action against an incompetent employee, even when such action is desperately needed. This law should be changed and replaced with a system that rewards excellence. A new system of employment contracts should be instituted which are subject to periodic renewals based on merit and excellent job performance. In truth, there is no need or justification for multi-year contracts for anyone paid from public funds.

Expand the Expertise

There are thousands of highly capable and talented men and women with experience and expertise in a variety of fields who would enjoy sharing their knowledge with our children. Who would be better qualified to teach about public finance than a retired banker, or who better to explain the intricacies of law than a retired judge? These and hundreds of people like them would love to share their lifetimes of knowledge with our children but they are forbidden from doing so by a law zealously defended by the teacher's union which feels their membership would be threatened by such a policy. It has been suggested from time to time that persons of achievement be invited and recruited to teach in our public schools, but each suggestion has been defeated by the teachers' union. An arrangement could be made so that these retired people could teach a few hours each day for a nominal hourly wage. Educators emphasize the importance of teachers who understand the process of teaching rather than being expert in the subjects they teach.

This is just one example of how a low-cost solution can be developed to improve the quality of our schools. As much sense as this suggestion makes, it hasn't been adopted because it is politically incorrect. The powerful teachers' union is fearful that such a personnel policy would dilute their influence and they are probably correct.

More Money Is Not The Answer

Billions have been poured into our public schools during the past three decades and only minimal progress has been made in raising student achievement. Even now, educators lobby for more taxpayer dollars while resisting meaningful reforms. Taxpayers are justified in their cynicism.

The school dropout problem has been cited as a major concern since more than 25 percent of our high school students leave before they graduate. In doing so, they burden our labor force with a surplus of unskilled workers. They also burden our prison system, in view of the grim statistic that 90 percent of all prison inmates are high school dropouts. People with skills to find productive jobs do so and become productive citizens.

A rather simple solution to the dropout problem would be for the General Assembly to enact legislation making the driver's license a privilege contingent upon successfully completing the requirements for a high school diploma. To enforce such a policy, the high school principal could be given authority equal to that of a parent for temporarily withdrawing a student's driving license when his or her school work declined. Just the threat of the loss of driving privileges would become a powerful incentive that translates into greater diligence in the classroom.

This suggestion has been made several times to the General Assembly but has failed to gain approval, ostensibly because it is politically unpopular.

Who Is Responsible For Our Low-Performing Schools?

A preponderance of school laws enacted in the past quarter century in this State has tended to benefit school employees rather than students. Could that be because school employees vote and children don't? In addition to just voting, one group of school employees, the teachers' union, contributes significantly to the politicians who support its policies. For those few legislators who vote "right" all the time, a massive grass roots effort to get out the vote can assure their election. Except for the two-year reign of Representative Joe Mavretic as Speaker of the House, which was engineered by a coalition of renegade Democrats and the Republicans, the teachers' union has been especially effective in getting the enthusiastic support of key House leaders who hold the committee chairmanships which influence public school legislation.

Nationwide, teacher union membership has grown from one percent in the early 1960s to 70 percent now. In North Carolina, the teachers' union boasts some 45,000 members. It is no coincidence that the growth of the teachers' union, and its success in influencing public school policy is a factor in the precipitous decline of student achievement.

What should we do? The answer is simple. It is not wrong that teachers should look out for what is in their best interest. That is the American way. However, the best interest of the teachers and other school employees should be balanced with a concern for what is best for the students.

It is not in the interest of students to protect the jobs of incompetent teachers. It is not in the best interest of students to fail to equip schools with high-tech computer labs and other state-of-the-art equipment which is necessary for our students to compete with the children of the world in developing survival skills for the 21st century.

It is not in the best interest of students to fail to set high performance standards because the teachers' union fears that higher standards would only embarrass schools more than they've already been embarrassed by years of failure and under achievement. Perhaps this is so in the short term, but in the long term, raising achievement standards is necessary before our schools can improve.

Again, the solution is simple. The General Assembly must change its priorities for our public schools. It should adopt a policy that puts the best interests of students first.

Higher Education

As good as our highly rated system of higher education is, it still needs improvement. There is too much duplication and redundancy among our public universities and community colleges.

Too many of the universities want to offer graduate programs even when there is little demand for such offerings. Too many of the community colleges are becoming unhappy with their role as vocational and technical training centers and want to become liberal arts institutions, feeding the four-year schools.

It may be that we ought to revise our public university system to designate a number of the institutions for freshmen and sophomores only and assign programs in the other institutions to educate juniors and seniors in their specialty fields. This proposed change shouldn't bother the professors since few of them teach underclassmen anyway. The State Auditor found that many of the professors employed at our public universities are reluctant to teach anybody, preferring instead to do research and write esoteric books and periodicals, perform outside consulting work and sit on corporate boards.

The community college system plays a vital role in preparing young men and women for skilled jobs. This is the mission the system was created to perform. Taxpayers should not be fooled by local community college leaders who mistakenly believe their schools will be held in higher esteem by abandoning this important mission.

RECOMMENDATION #3

Eliminate federal mandates. Federal mandates have become a heavy burden for state and local governments nationwide, particularly in poor and rural counties. A federal mandate is the term that characterizes mandated expenditures passed on to state and local governments by the federal government. In all cases of the mandates, state and local governments had no say in the adoption of the programs which were established by Congress. In many cases, mandated programs were not even debated thoroughly by Congress but were crafted largely by bureaucrats and advocates of special interests. Yet, their costs are passed on in the form of higher local taxes to taxpayers who have no say in the operation of the programs. As well-intentioned as these programs are, they are destroying the fiscal fabric of our country.

Take Medicaid, for example. This program was created in the mid-1970s to provide health care for the poor. More than one million North Carolinians received Medicaid assistance in 1994. When the Medicaid program first began, a total of 455,000 North Carolinians were enrolled as eligible. The number of Medicaid beneficiaries actually declined during the next decade, reaching a low of 408,000 in 1983, but then the program began a precipitous climb. In just one year, between 1990 and 1991, some 125,000 new Medicaid eligibles were added. Total Medicaid spending has tripled in the five years prior to 1993. The federal government provides 65 percent of the cost of this program, in money borrowed from future taxpayers. The State's share is 20 percent and the county's share is 15 percent. In 1993, North Carolina's Medicaid bill was $700 million. And the counties had to come up with another $525 million for their share of a program which State and local voters have never had a say in how it was created and operated.

Unlike the federal government, State and local governments cannot defer their tax bills to citizens yet unborn. That leaves leaders with the unpleasant choice of either taking the money away from other public programs or raising taxes. Often, the easy choice is to take funding away from other programs, including education, public safety and crime prevention. Often there is no choice at all.

Take the hypothetical case of a Medicaid patient from a poor, rural county who has just received a heart transplant at a cost of $500,000. The State and county share of this expenditure is $100,000 for the State and $75,000 for the county. For several of our small counties, it takes two cents of the tax rate to raise that amount of property taxes. And that is just to pay for one person's medical bill.

To be sure this is a program which benefits many people, but is it a program that we can afford and would our elected officials have voted for it had they been given the chance to do so? Also, remember that a primary consequence of the publicly funded medical care program is that it represents a massive transfer of wealth from taxpayers to the providers of medical care.

The solution to federal mandates is for public leaders at both the State and local levels to stand up to the people who represent us in Congress and tell them we've had enough. North Carolina should consider joining other states that are mounting legal challenges to the concept of mandates. The argument that federally mandated expenditures are not consistent with the intent of the 10th Amendment, which reserves the powers not specifically given the federal government for the states, is a valid argument. Certainly, there is nothing in the constitution which says that the federal government has the power to enact a massive health care program and pass the costs along to state and local governments.

Mandates have become a form of national madness and unless we curtail them, they will consume us all.

RECOMMENDATION #4

Refocus economic development. North Carolina spends more than $100 million a year recruiting new industry and encouraging existing businesses and firms to create more jobs. Governor Luther Hodges is credited with inventing the business of industrial recruitment in North Carolina, for which he was at first criticized. The Research Triangle Park, with its some 40,000 high-tech and high paying jobs is a testament to the visionary leadership of Governor Hodges.

We did a marvelous job during the 1970s and early 1980s promoting North Carolina as a good place to do business. We are still trying to emulate that success; however, the kinds of jobs we were successful in attracting a decade ago are no longer interested in North Carolina. They are going to Mexico and to the Pacific Rim where labor is cheaper.

The competition for the high-tech jobs which flocked to the Research Triangle Park a decade ago has gotten intense as other states have recognized the benefits of this kind of business.

The failure of our public school system to educate students so they can move directly into the workplace with basic math and verbal skills has caught up with us and is keeping good jobs away.

Our cheap labor, which was once a major incentive for luring industry here, is now not cheap enough since workers elsewhere will work for even less.

And, quite frankly, we have outdone ourselves in offering "incentives" to firms to locate here. We became a master at putting together attractive packages of taxpayer-subsidized incentives in the late 1970s and early 1980s which were effective in giving us bragging rights as the leading industry recruiter for many years. Other states quickly caught on. Alabama beat us badly in 1993 getting Mercedes-Benz to build a plant there instead of here. Alabama did that by offering nearly a half billion dollars in taxpayer incentives in tax forgiveness, worker training programs, land, and with a big Mercedes sign on top of the football scoreboard at the University of Alabama. We were embarrassed by the loss of the Mercedes plant because company officials narrowed down their final three locations to North Carolina, South Carolina and Alabama, in a strategy calculated to generate an all-out bidding war to see which state would give the most away to get this plant.

For the long term, North Carolina taxpayers are probably better off that we did not get the plant here. It is doubtful that the average, poor taxpayer in Alabama will ever get the full benefit from the Mercedes plant that he has paid for, reported to be close to a half billion dollars.

We will have to reinvent the process of economic development in North Carolina if we are to create good jobs for our high school and college graduates.

The Global TransPark being developed at Kinston is an example of forward thinking by State leaders which can create opportunities for the future. This concept of developing a major new air cargo port, although an experiment, offers great promise to the farmers of eastern North Carolina as they seek to replace the income that will be lost from the crop of tobacco in the coming years. The Global TransPark offers a great opportunity for getting farm produce to the lucrative markets in the northeast, which are no more than an hour away by air. Fresh farm produce from the fields of North Carolina can become a reality in the markets of Washington, D.C., Baltimore, Philadelphia, New York and other major, east coast, urban areas.

RECOMMENDATION #5

Make government more participatory. Citizens have indicated in different ways, but emphatically in recent years, that they want to participate in the process of government to a greater degree than ever before.

The rise of participatory government means the decline of representative government. The General Assembly must recognize that as voters become better informed, and as they become more disenchanted with the failure, real or perceived, of government programs to work as they are intended, and as they have been promised, voters are going to become more involved.

One solution to this problem would be to allow North Carolina citizens to initiate proposed constitutional amendments through the voter initiative process, as voters now can do in almost half the other states. This would be a very simple thing to do. The General Assembly should permit North Carolina citizens the opportunity to force a vote on a proposed amendment to our constitution by obtaining a certain number of signatures on a petition. There should be, of course, a substantial number of signatures required in order to screen out frivolous or narrowly supported measures. Five percent of the total number of voters taking part in the most recent Presidential general election would be a reasonable threshold.

The debate over giving veto power to the Governor is a good example of how the voter initiative would make North Carolina government more democratic. Although polls have shown for more than a decade that voters approve of the veto and the Senate has voted to place the issue on the ballot, the Speaker of the House has successfully kept the issue from being put to a vote by the people of North Carolina. This is clearly an issue which the people ought to decide, not one powerful politician in the General Assembly.

Also, the General Assembly should keep its promises. When the corporate income tax was raised in 1991, business leaders were promised that this would be only temporary and the increase would be rescinded once the economy improved. The economy improved so much by the time the General Assembly convened in the summer of 1994 for the short budget session that they had more than $1.2 billion of "surplus" revenue to spend. Yet, they were still unwilling to rescind the tax increase as they had promised. This kind of behavior only breeds further cynicism among taxpayers.

The time has come also to give North Carolina voters another effective tool for making public officials accountable—the recall initiative. There ought to be an authorized procedure, and this could be done with legislation, for citizens to initiate with a petition and a sufficient number of signatures the recall of a public official who has abused his or her trust. All publicly elected officials at both the state and local levels of government should be subject to recall by voters.

Government ought to be more "user friendly." Have you approached a typical government agency for assistance or information? Unless you already know specifically to whom your inquiry should be targeted you will probably have to make a half dozen or more phone calls just to find the right person with whom to speak.

There is the mistaken idea among too many public employees that citizens and taxpayers are a problem to be dealt with, and as a result, the typical response that an ordinary citizen gets from a government employee is one of neglect, disinterest or even discourtesy. That must change.

RECOMMENDATION #6

Equalize the balance of power. When North Carolina's founding fathers crafted our government, they intentionally created a powerful legislature and a weak executive branch. They did this because they wanted to spare future generations from having to deal with tyrannical governors such as the abusive royal governors appointed by the King of England.

For more than two centuries, North Carolina's General Assembly has been all powerful in setting State policy, raising taxes and spending them, and in making the laws by which we have to abide. That is because the Governor of North Carolina does not have the power to veto actions by the General Assembly. He is the only Governor not to have the veto power and because of this shortcoming, our Governor is considered to be one of the weakest governors in America.

Polls have indicated for some time that North Carolina voters would like for their chief executive to have the veto. The Senate has approved an amendment to the State constitution which would allow voters to choose. However, the House of Representatives has refused to allow voters the chance to express their wish.

It is time for the General Assembly to put this matter to a vote by the people.

Giving the Governor the veto would result in better legislation because it would force the General Assembly to consider the broader public interest rather than be influenced so much by a few powerful special interests.

Giving the Governor the veto would make him or her a stronger and better leader. With the veto, the Governor would be forced to take positions on issues which he now can avoid. The power of the veto would make good governors better and it would expose weak governors for what they are.

RECOMMENDATION #7

Make government work. Cynicism about today's government runs deep among our people. Nothing short of a major change in the way government works will reverse this trend and re-establish the faith which is needed for the republic to survive.

People want their government to work. Citizens know that it costs money to provide public services. However, they are also keenly aware when government programs fail. The press has done an excellent job of exposing government waste and inefficiency and this is a useful public service by the news media.

Government leaders must take the initiative to improve the quality of their work so that the trust and faith of the citizens served by government will be restored.

The General Assembly should revisit the process by which it spends the public's money. It seems to have labored under the misguided belief that it must spend all the tax revenue available in good times and then declare a crisis so that voters will support a tax increase in bad times.

Voters have a role to play too–to become informed about the various government programs, to know what programs should accomplish and whether or not they are working. Then, voters must hold their elected representatives in the General Assembly, and all public officeholders, accountable for what they say and for what they do.

In Conclusion

Drastic change is needed in the way North Carolina government works in order to regain citizen confidence. To preserve our democratic process, we must hold the faith and confidence of the people we serve and the people who pay taxes. Otherwise, they will withhold their support and the republic will perish.

If it seems that I dwell too long on the subject of education, and perhaps risk criticism for having dealt too much with the negatives of this important public challenge, let me justify that decision. Education has commanded the largest portion of our State budget for many years. Improving our public schools has been our top State priority for nearly half a century. The taxpayer has certainly done his part and is being asked to do more. Yet something is wrong when in the face of drastically increasing public expenditures for public education, we do not see significant improvement in student achievement.

The impact upon our future public finances in North Carolina of low-performing public schools, in the wake of higher and higher education budgets, is profound. Over-crowded prisons and increased drug abuse are just two of the problems which result from an inferior education system. Both of these are very expensive problems for society. We must improve our schools and we must get a better return on our investment in public education in the future than we've gotten in the past.

The choice for us now, while we still have time, is to restructure our public spending so that tax funded programs will work as they are intended and that government will begin to serve the public purpose as it is supposed to do.

Chapter 2

Portrait of a Modern State Profile: North Carolina

At various times in its history, North Carolina has been called the "Rip Van Winkle State," the "Dixie Dynamo," a "militant mediocracy" and "progressive." The truth about who we are and what we are lies somewhere in between, or perhaps is a combination of all these contradictory and complimentary characteristics. We are a people and a State in transition.

If Dr. Elisha Mitchell, the scientist, visionary explorer, and publisher of the State's first geologic survey, were alive today to stand at the summit of his beloved Mount Mitchell, the highest peak in eastern America, and assess the State beneath him, he would see a place and a people far different from the way it was two and one-half centuries ago when the first settlers arrived and began carving their villages and towns out of the vast wilderness.

Today, there are 6,903,946 North Carolinians, a substantial increase from the first census in 1790 which counted just 394,000 citizens who called North Carolina home. It was then the third most populated colony out of thirteen. Today, we are 10th among the fifty states in population and 28th in land area.

We rank in the top one-fifth of American states in total bank deposits and among the bottom five in wages our workers earn.

We are first in the nation in the production of tobacco and near the bottom in taxing this crop which just three decades ago accounted for four-fifths of all farm income. Today, tobacco generates more than $1 billion annually but that is only one-fifth of our cash farm income.

We rank near the top in the quality of our splendid public university system but near the bottom in the achievement of our public schools. We have arguably the best public maintained system of highways in the nation, leading some to say North Carolina has the best roads to the worst schools in the nation.

We rank low in marriages but high in divorces.

North Carolina is a State in transition. It is a good place to live, as evidenced by the thousands of people who move here each year, retreating from America's congested, crime-infested cities whose escalating budgets are leading to higher and higher taxes and deteriorating public services.

The fact that so many people are voting with their presence is reassuring; however, there are alarming signs that signal a chorus of concern that all is not well and we should chart a new course. There is much that we can do to make better use of our public resources and to improve the quality of life for our citizens.

Here is a capsulated look at our Tar Heel State today.[1]

Geography

The geography of North Carolina has determined to a large extent its growth and development. The absence of deepwater ports dictated migration patterns from Virginia, Charleston, Savannah, and ports of the north, rather than arrivals disembarking directly.

Most suitable for agriculture, the coastal plain has always been dominated by a farm economy. This region with its large, flat and fertile fields, was once home to hundreds of large plantations which grew most of the State's cotton and bright leaf tobacco.

The yeoman farmers settled in both the coastal plain and the red clay hills of the piedmont where they cleared small farms from the wilderness. Limited by the capacity of their own toil, they conceived large families, hoping for a bountiful supply of helpful hands to assist with the chores and daily tasks necessary to survive.

The people who made it to the Blue Ridge highlands were a hardy folk, a characteristic necessary for surviving the harsh winters and for eking out a meager living. The small amount of bottom land has always been a barrier to farming and in recent years has limited the availability of industrial jobs.

Geographic Regions

North Carolina is divided into three distinct regions: the coastal plain, the piedmont and the mountains.

The coastal plain extends from the Atlantic Ocean to the fall line, generally just west of Interstate 95, where the elevation rises to about 500 feet. This is the State's largest region with 45 percent of the total area.

[1]Statistics in this chapter are extracted in part from: State Data Center, *Statistical Abstract of North Carolina Counties, 1991* (Raleigh, North Carolina: Office of State Budget and Management), various tables; *U.S. Census Reports*, various issues; and, Kathleen O'Leary Morgan, Scott Morgan and Neal Quitno, eds., *State Rankings 1992, A Statistical View of the 50 United States* (Lawrence, Kansas: Morgan Quitno Corporation, 1992), various tables.

The piedmont, with 43 percent of the total area, is the State's most heavily industrialized and most densely populated region. The piedmont extends from the fall line to the foothills which rise to 1,500 feet at the eastern edge of the Blue Ridge Mountains.

The mountains comprise the State's smallest region, accounting for only about 12 percent of the total land area. It extends some 200 miles from Virginia to the Georgia border and is bounded along the entire way by Tennessee. The mountains rise abruptly beginning at the western edge of the piedmont to elevations of from 1,500 to 2,000 feet and include the tallest mountains of eastern America. More than a dozen peaks soar above 6,000 feet. Mount Mitchell, at 6,684 feet, is the highest mountain east of the Mississippi River.

For the first hundred years of our history, most of the State's wealth lay in the coastal plain, generated by the crops of cotton and tobacco on the large plantations. In turn, the holders of this wealth dominated the social, political and cultural affairs of North Carolina during its formative years. They did this through their control of the General Assembly which shaped the State's early tax and finance policies to the advantage of the wealthy planters.

Today, farming is still an important part of the economy of eastern North Carolina; however, industry has begun to dot the flat fields and to pay the bills.

The concentration of industry has grown mostly in the densely populated piedmont, particularly the piedmont crescent which extends roughly along Interstate 85 from Raleigh to Charlotte. Textile mills were once drawn to this region because of cheap labor and cheap water power. The mills attracted poor farmers who found it more and more difficult to extract even a meager living from the red clay soil, as the land's nutrients were depleted by decades of poor farm practices. In recent years modern industry has found a favorable climate for doing business in this region.

Tourism thrives in all three regions, but with greatest flourish along the oceanfront resorts and in the high mountains. Tourism also prospers in the Sandhills, famous for great golf courses and mild winters.

Social

The English first settled in Jamestown and as others came, they spread out into the wilderness to the west and to the south. They were industrious and hardworking people, qualities necessary for surviving the unforgiving frontiers. Among this group were few aristocrats, but rather the seeds of what would become the great mass of American settlers, the stable, upwardly mobile middle class.

The independent Scots arrived in droves through the port at Wilmington and moved up the Cape Fear, settling along the South Carolina border as well. The Scotch-Irish, too, found their love of liberty and deeply religious tradition in conflict with the plantation way of life that dominated the early coastal plain. They arrived through the port of Philadelphia during the second quarter of the 18th century and followed a path marked by the foothills of the Allegheny Mountains until they settled on their small, red clay farms of the piedmont and the foothills of North Carolina. Another parade of the Scotch-Irish arrived at the port of Charleston and moved up the valleys of the Yadkin, the Catawba and the Broad Rivers until they converged on settlements peopled by their kin from Philadelphia.

Early German settlers moved down from Pennsylvania and established several communities in the western piedmont, one of which they called Salem. The community later merged with the town of Winston and became the city of Winston-Salem. Their love of learning and their skill as craftsmen gave birth to one of the first high-tech centers in early America. The Germans, or Moravians, were thrifty, industrious and intelligent. They had running water in their homes at the time of the American Revolution and were perhaps the only people in North Carolina to enjoy such a luxury.

Early North Carolina was populated by a blend of European immigrants who came in search of opportunity and Africans brought against their will.

The emergence of cotton as king of the southern plantation in the 19th Century inspired one of the ugliest chapters of American history—the era of slave trade. Young blacks were captured in their native Africa, often with the aid of their village rulers and brought here to provide what was mistakenly thought to be a cheap source of labor. Though the foreign slave trade was abolished in 1808, the domestic practice of buying and selling slaves flourished for more than another half century. The misguided slave trade has become one of our nation's costliest mistakes. It is a part of our past that haunts us today resulting in racial strife, discord and rancor that lingers more than 130 years after slavery was abolished.

In 1860, as the Civil War began, there were 311,000 slaves and some 30,000 free African American people in North Carolina out of a total population of 993,000. And, there were 1,168 native Americans. Most of the slaves were kept on the large plantations concentrated in the eastern third of the State. Today, several counties which were once home to these large plantations have majority black populations.

Climate

North Carolina's climate is one of its great natural resources. Four distinct seasons are a plus. Winters are short and mild in much of the State, except for the mountains which have exploited the frequent snowfalls into a prosperous ski industry. The long, hot and humid summers have supported a healthy agricultural economy from the early days of settlement.

In the spring and summer, the bursts of blooms from a great variety of flowers, both wild and cultivated, transform the State into a great and beautiful garden. In the fall, the radiant reds and the brilliant yellows of the changing deciduous forests tell the passing of another season.

The factors which contribute to such a favorable climate are, of course, the gift of a provident Creator. Our location in the middle latitudes, equivalent to the Mediterranean, is adjacent to the Atlantic Ocean on the east and protected in the west by high mountains, which tend to dissipate the brunt of harsh winter storms–all of which are favorable factors.

An average rainfall of 50 inches, distributed fairly uniformly through the year, is yet another favorable climatic factor which contributes both to a strong economy and an enjoyable place to live.

Area

North Carolina is comprised of 52,662 square miles, 4,000 square miles of which is water, making it the nation's 28th largest state. Sampson County (963 square miles) is the State's largest. Chowan County with just 172 square miles is the smallest county.

Population

Of the State's 6.6 million people in 1990, five million were white, 1.5 million were African-American and 100,000 belonged to other races.

North Carolina gains some 40,000 people a year by migration.

In the 1990 census, we became an urban society for the first time in our history as 50.4 percent of our people were found to live in urban areas versus 49.6 percent rural inhabitants. Just two decades earlier rural residents of the State outnumbered city dwellers by nearly a half million.

The urban residents share less than three percent of North Carolina's total land area.

There are 1.6 million families, 813,000 with children. Single parent households headed by females totaled 130,000 as compared to just 18,000 with male heads.

The 1980 census found 2.3 million housing units, two-thirds of which were occupied by owners and one-third by renters. There were 222,000 mobile homes. Substandard housing units totaled 161,000. Nearly 600,000 housing units are more than 40 years old and some 350,000 are 50 years old.

The average number of people per household in 1985 was 2.64 and declining. It was 3.25 in 1970.

There were 2.6 million North Carolinians married in 1980 and what they told the census takers represents somewhat of a dilemma. There were 8,000 more married men than women. How could that be? But then women caught up in the divorce category, outnumbering men by 40,000.

There are some 140,000 pregnancies each year, 27,000 of them among teenagers. Abortions totaled 35,000 in 1989.

There were 105,000 live births in 1990, not a major increase from the 98,000 recorded in 1970. Resident deaths totaled 57,000 in 1989, 18,000 non-geriatric. Violent deaths totaled 4,779 in 1989 as compared with just 220 less in 1980.

There were 1,171 infant deaths in 1989 giving North Carolina the dubious claim as having the highest ratio of infant mortality in America. More than 8,000 low-weight babies are born each year resulting in high infant mortality rates and expensive medical care. A large number of the low weight babies are the result of poverty, ignorance, neglect or a combination of these factors.

There were 51,000 marriages and 32,000 divorces in 1989. North Carolina ranks 42 in the ratio of marriages per 1,000 population and eighth in divorces.

Great Tar Heels

North Carolina is a place, as is written in our State song, "where the weak grow strong and the strong grow great." Many native-born citizens have risen to great achievement and prominence. The Reverend Billy Graham has preached the gospel to millions. With the aid of modern communications he has ministered to the spiritual needs of more people than any other religious leader in the entire history of man.

Michael Jordan, once cut from his high school basketball team, overcame that minor obstacle to become America's most celebrated and highest paid athlete. Boxing greats Floyd Patterson and Sugar Ray Leonard began their lives here.

The vision of great leaders of the past lingers today to lift our spirits and inspire us to higher achievements. Archibald Murphey, from Hillsborough, first challenged his fellow legislators to provide public schools for all children. Governor Zebulon Vance was a sturdy rock during the Civil War and kept the State from suffering even more during this low point in our history.

Governor Charles Aycock, elected in 1900 as the Democrats regained control of State government, became the great champion of public schools. During his term in office, a new school was built each day. They were, in many cases, small, one-room school houses which cost less to build then than a single tire on today's school bus costs. But they were each a beacon of hope, letting the light of learning shine through the State's backwoods. Governors Cameron Morrison and W. Kerr Scott are remembered for their ambitious roadbuilding programs which literally got farmers out of the mud and led to an effective system of farm-to-market roads. These roads not only spurred agriculture but have become a major factor in developing a strong industrial economy.

In our shrine for great achievers, there must be a place for U.S. Senator Sam Ervin, Jr. His keen intellect and folksy sense of humor prevailed in the mid-1970s as he presided over the Senate Watergate Committee investigating the misdeeds of a President who chose to resign in disgrace rather than face almost certain impeachment.

Three North Carolinians rose from the good Tar Heel soil to become President. They were Andrew Jackson, Andrew Johnson and James Polk. However, our claim to their greatness is limited since each of them left North Carolina at an early age and went to Tennessee. From there they rose in stature and rank to the highest office in the land. Only one Tar Heel has ever become Speaker of the U.S. House of Representatives and that was the parsimonious Nathaniel Macon of Warren County. He was a member of the U.S. House of Representatives for 24 years, serving six years as Speaker, from 1801 to 1807, and then he served 12 years in the U.S. Senate.

Few American writers have risen higher in public esteem than Asheville's Thomas Wolfe, the troubled poet who charmed America for a decade with his beautiful prose and then died in the prime of his life. There have been other Tar Heel wordsmiths who excelled with the pen. Among them, O. Henry and Paul Green.

Andy Griffith has entertained for a generation with his simple sense of humor. Ava Gardner charmed us with her beauty and others who found prominence on the silver screen from North Carolina were Vincent Price and Randolph Scott.

No television journalist has ever set a higher standard of public achievement than our own Edward R. Murrow, though two other Tar Heels, David Brinkley and Charles Kuralt, have come close. Native sons Clifton Daniels and Gene Roberts have held the exalted position as editor of the *New York Times*. And, Vermont Royster did the same at the the *Wall Street Journal.*

Health Care

In 1989 there were 4,457 primary health physicians (as compared with 12,163 lawyers), 1,223 mid-level practitioners; 44,355 registered nurses and 2,663 dentists.

Hospital beds totaled 48,000 with 21,000 categorized as general and 27,000 as skilled and intermediate care. There were 732,000 hospital discharges. Some 176,000 people were treated for substance abuse in 1990.

Public Assistance

The number of welfare recipients more than quadrupled between 1970 and 1990, increasing from 101,000 to 408,000. In 1989 there were 765,000 North Carolinians enrolled in the Medicaid program, which pays the medical bills of the poor.

Social Security

More than 1 million people in North Carolina get Social Security checks. There are 642,000 retired workers and some 97,000 disabled persons between the ages of 16 and 64 receiving benefits.

Education

Higher education is one of our great achievements. Enrollment in the State's excellent public colleges and universities almost doubled between 1970 and 1990, to some 102,000 students. The 16-campus State university system ranks as one of the nation's best. Private college enrollment in 37 independent and privately supported colleges and universities in

1989 totaled 30,000. Some 18 percent of North Carolinians have college degrees.

One of the most remarkable education success stories in North Carolina is that of our excellent community colleges. In just three decades community college enrollment has soared to more than 330,000 full-time and part-time students seeking to acquire job skills. A recent study found that graduates of these down-to-earth institutions of higher learning find jobs more readily than graduates of the State's four-year liberal arts schools, and many community college graduates start work with higher pay.

Public Schools

Not many superlatives are justified, however, in describing our system of public schools which ranked 48th in the nation in 1993 in the SAT scores of its rising high school seniors. That is the same ranking our schools were given in 1900, at a time when there were only 48 states.[2]

The dilemma for our public schools is real. Taxpayers have been pressed hard to fund increased expenditures; yet, meaningful changes in the way our schools are managed and operated have been made reluctantly, if at all.

Economic

Some 3.4 million Tar Heels were gainfully employed in 1990, 2.9 million of them in non-agricultural jobs. The total annual payroll in 1988 was $45.2 billion. The median family income was $16,792.

Total personal income among North Carolinians in 1993 was $127 billion and the per capita income was $18,444.

There were 158,000 business establishments, 90 percent of them classified as small, having between one and 19 employees.

Some 11,000 manufacturing establishments employ a total of 863,000 people.

Retail establishments totaled 43,000, with gross retail sales in 1990 of $65 billion, nearly double the $34 billion recorded a decade earlier and more than a five-fold increase from the $12 billion reported in 1970.

There were 12,382 finance, insurance and real estate establishments.

Black-owned businesses totaled 17,692 firms and women owned more than 93,000 firms.

[2]Samuel Huntington Hobbs, Jr., *North Carolina, Economic and Social* (Chapel Hill: The University of North Carolina Press, 1930), 250.

Millions of visitors come to North Carolina each year to spend leisure time in America's veritable "Variety Vacationland" and to pursue business ventures. In the process, they spend more than $8 billion annually, making the State's travel and tourism industry one of the most prosperous economic sectors. This industry provides jobs for some 250,000 people.

Agriculture

Farming has always been an important way of life. From the first days of the Colony, until as recently as a generation ago, the family farm in North Carolina was a major source of sustenance for the typical family.

Farm income is still important, accounting for a total of $5.2 billion in gross revenue in 1992. This was triple the $1.5 billion gross farm income reported in 1970. While farm income has increased sharply, the number of farms and farmers has steadily dwindled. In 1970, for example, the State's farm population was estimated at 530,000. That number had decreased to just 188,000 in 1980, and it shrank again to 117,000 in 1990.

In 1925, North Carolina had more farms (283,495) than any other state in the nation except Texas, which was five times larger. That number had diminished by 75 percent by 1993 to just 59,000 farms. North Carolina farms have disappeared from the Tar Heel landscape, even during the period that our own native born and bred Jesse Helms presided as Chairman of the Agriculture Committee of the United States Senate. Even as the number of farms declined, the number of bureaucrats in the U.S. Department of Agriculture grew. The average farm is 159 acres and total farmland in the State is 9.4 million acres, less than half of which is harvested.

Still, the average North Carolina farmer is better off than his counterpart throughout the nation. In 1992, the average gross income per North Carolina farm was $101,000 as compared to $94,000 nationally. And the net income per North Carolina farm was $41,000, compared with only $23,000 nationally.

Tobacco is the State's leading cash crop, as it has been since 1919, accounting for $1 billion in cash income during 1992. Broilers are second ($856 million), hogs third ($730 million) and turkeys fourth ($475 million). North Carolina leads the nation in the production of tobacco, sweet potatoes and turkeys. It is second in cucumbers, trout, poultry products and hogs.

Farmers and their leaders are deeply concerned about how to replace the income from tobacco, which represents one-fifth of all farm income. In the wake of mounting public criticism concerning tobacco use as a major cause of health problems and deaths, the demise of tobacco is as certain as the fall of cotton a century ago.

There is much good news in the gains experienced by trout farmers, chicken and turkey growers, and the cultivators of blueberries and strawberries. These are healthy foods, sought by a rapidly increasing, diet-conscious population.

North Carolina farmers rank third or fourth nationally in the production of more than 30 different commodities such as peanuts, blueberries, pecans, eggs, rye, cotton, grapes, tomatoes, soybeans, Irish potatoes, corn, peaches, winter wheat, oats, barley, milk, cattle and hay.

Though the farm population has grown smaller in the 20th century, its economic influence has grown larger as the farmer, aided by high-tech equipment and modern planting and cultivating measures, has become highly efficient. Much of the credit for this progress goes to my longtime friend and mentor, Commissioner of Agriculture, James Allen Graham, who was appointed to that job in 1964 and has provided strong leadership to the State's farmers for three decades.[3]

Wealth

The wealth of a state is its people. If the people of the State's wealthiest county were to be switched with the people of the poorest county, everything else remaining the same, within a decade the fortunes of the two counties would also switch. While wealth is measured directly in the form of money, natural and manmade resources and other tangible assets, the ultimate wealth of a place is the ability of its people to obtain money through their intellect and skill.

Education, health, history, heritage, culture, natural resources and prevalent attitudes of a people are factors which determine how they value wealth, accumulate it and preserve it. One of the great strengths of North Carolina is that while it is not a place of abundant wealth, its thrifty people have a history of making the most of limited resources.

Income

Total personal income in 1993 was $129.8 billion, an increase of 1,500

[3] North Carolina Department of Agriculture, *1993 North Carolina Agricultural Statistics*, various tables.

percent in three decades. The average annual wage in 1990 was $20,220 (ranking 36) and the average hourly wage was $9.22, ranking 46. Only workers in South Carolina, Arkansas, South Dakota and Mississippi earned less.

Gross retail sales in 1990 were $65 billion, a five-fold increase since 1970. Value added by manufacture in 1987 was $47 billion. The gross state product in 1989 was $130 billion, ranking 12th among the 50 states.

Taxes

Total state and local revenue generated in 1993 was $16.8 billion, ranking North Carolina 13th in the nation. Total federal taxes collected from North Carolinians by the Internal Revenue Service in 1993 was $29 billion. That figure did not include the $18 billion paid by North Carolina workers and their employers in Social Security taxes. The State ranks fourth in motor fuel tax revenue.

Bank Deposits

The total assets of North Carolina's 63 State and National banks in 1993 was $96.6 billion, ranking 11th among the 50 states. That is a 10-fold increase in assets from just two decades ago. And, it represents a decrease by one-third in the number of independent banks during the same period of time. The number of branch banks has remained about the same at 1,022.

Insurance

The value of insurance premiums reported in 1993 was $10.9 billion.

Property

The tax value of real and personal property totaled $288.7 billion in 1993 and yielded $2 billion in local property taxes.

Debt

Nowhere is the frugal nature of North Carolina's people more evident than in the matter of public debt. Our total State and local debt in the form of general obligation bonds was $5.1 billion as of June 30, 1993, and was one of the lowest amounts of public debt by any state. In 1990, we ranked 48th in the nation in the amount of per capita State debt ($84) and our per capita combined State and local debt was $742.

Transportation

Good roads have become not only the State's great source of pride but also its catalyst for growth. North Carolina leads the nation in the number of state-maintained public roads. Its 77,000 miles of public roads are the envy of the nation and have contributed greatly to a better life for all citizens. They are funded by a 21.3 cents per gallon gasoline tax, the fourth highest such tax in the nation.

The automobile is the principal means of transportation. Tar Heel citizens owned 5.9 million motor vehicles in 1993.

Air transportation is becoming increasingly important in business and inter-state travel. Raleigh and Charlotte leaders are proud of the airport hubs and the international flights originating in their cities; however, the financial difficulty encountered by all major airlines during the 1990s has placed the future of air travel in great uncertainty. Greensboro was becoming a major airport hub in the mid-1990s.

Politics

There are 4,888,882 people in the State old enough to vote; however, only 3.4 million of them are registered to vote. Fewer than two-thirds of those eligible ever bother to vote. Seldom do as many as half of all the registered voters take the trouble to do so. During the 1994 primary election, only 15 percent of those eligible to vote did. In 1990, there were 2.1 million registered Democrats and one million Republicans. However, those numbers are deceiving, in view of the fact that Republican governors have served as the State's chief executive in 12 of the 20 years between 1972 and 1992. Republicans have held one of North Carolina's two U.S. Senate seats for the entire 22 years leading up to 1994 and the other seat for 10 of those years.

North Carolinians voted for only one Republican Presidential candidate in this century before 1972, and that was Herbert Hoover in 1928 who was running against the unpopular Catholic, Al Smith. Since 1972 North Carolinians have voted for only one Democrat and that was fellow southerner Jimmy Carter in 1976. Even the regional ties of native Arkansan Bill Clinton were not strong enough for Democrats to prevail in the 1992 Presidential election.

North Carolina voters have been a conservative lot since the beginning of the Republic and there is no reason to believe they are changing their feelings today. After a tumultuous Reconstruction period during which they were out of power much of the time, Democrats gained control of North Carolina politics in 1900 with the election of Charles Brantley Aycock as governor. They maintained control of State government for nearly three-quarters of a century, until 1972.

As the Democratic Party has departed from its traditional, conservative heritage, a trend which began in the 1960s, the party has consistently lost favor among North Carolina voters and its power base continues to erode.

Crime

Crime has become a major problem, as it has in the rest of the nation. Our crime problem is a real and growing threat to the safety and security of our citizens. The North Carolina crime index, which is a composite of the crimes committed by and against citizens, increased 40 percent during the 1980s.

There were 36,000 violent crimes committed in North Carolina in 1989, an increase of 40 percent since 1980. Property crimes increased 25 percent, to 305,000. There are nearly a half million arrests each year and some 75,000 people are on probation.

There were 9,954 substantiated reports of child abuse in 1990.

Prison admissions doubled between 1970 and 1990 to 21,800. The implication of this statistic is far reaching in that our prisons can only accommodate 22,000 inmates. If we are admitting the equivalent of our total capacity each year, then we are releasing a huge number of criminals back into society well before their sentences have been served. Our prisons have become a revolving door, as criminals go in one day, sentenced to long terms and come out a few months later. Prison is no longer a deterrent but rather an occupational hazard and is looked upon by professional criminals as just another risk of doing business.

We spend as much ($24 million) a year paying lawyers to defend indigent persons accused of criminal conduct as we do to operate the district attorney offices which are charged with the duty of prosecuting all crimes.

We rank, among the other states, consistent with our population size in most crimes, higher in assault and burglary, lower in robbery. Of the 23,438 murders committed in the United States in 1990, some 552 were in North Carolina, giving us the dubious rank of tenth in the nation.

It costs more than $24,000 a year to keep a person in prison. That is four times the amount we spend on the average student enrolled in our public schools and four times the cost of sending a student to our public university system.

Summary

If Dr. Mitchell could stand today at the top of his beloved mountain and look down upon the changes which have taken place in the State he once surveyed on foot, he would see a state of many contrasts and conflicts. Some might say he would actually see two different North Carolinas.

The people with whom Dr. Mitchell associated in the early 1800s were hard-working, God-fearing, law-abiding, thrifty, industrious and delighted for the opportunity to carve a new civilization out of the wilderness. Their descendants have thrived here and comprise four-fifths of the State's population, which remains hard-working, law-abiding, thrifty and industrious—diligent men and women whose main goal is to see that their children have a chance for a better life.

North Carolina today is still the beautiful place it always has been, the verdant, veritable "Variety Vacationland." Located on the east coast, almost in the center of the nation's population concentration, North Carolina has easy and convenient access to America's most lucrative markets for its farm and industrial products. It is still, for many, a land of opportunity.

But, Dr. Mitchell would also see a growing underclass, unable, and often unwilling, to care for themselves, increasingly dependent upon public assistance programs for their food, shelter and comfort.

To be sure, many among us have prospered. Those who have taken advantage of the great educational opportunities now find themselves in the fast lane of the much-heralded information highway with good, high paying jobs and the promise of a secure future.

In spite of the billions of taxpayer dollars we've spent on education, one of five North Carolinians is still illiterate and poor, possessing little hope of ever improving his station in life.

The most pressing concern of the 1990s is that the fastest growing part of the State budget is public assistance. As hard as we've tried to eliminate poverty and ignorance, we have failed. Instead, we have spawned a system that traps victims of poverty in an endless cycle of bureaucratic red tape, despair and hopelessness. The bureaucracy that we created to rescue people from poverty has, in fact, done just the opposite. It has imposed regulations which have wrecked the family and encouraged teenage mothers to have babies. Programs that we conceived to relieve misery have compounded the problem they once set out to solve. The burden of paying for these misguided efforts now threatens to overwhelm the capacity of the hard-working middle class to pay for them. In North Carolina, as elsewhere in the nation, this is one of the things we must change.

Chapter 3

The Treasurers 1784-1994

North Carolina's twenty-five Treasurers comprise a unique group of public servants. Patience, perseverance, endurance and integrity are qualities which they shared. Most of them possessed a genuine love for North Carolina and a devotion for its people that was reflected in the care with which they guarded the public purse during their terms of office.

During the early days of the Carolina Colony, a Treasurer's Court was established, beginning in 1669, to handle public money. The office of Treasurer was created by the legislature and appointments to the office were filled by the lower house of the Colonial Assembly. Between 1740 and 1779 there was one treasurer for each of the Northern and Southern Districts. Four additional treasurers were added in 1779 for a total of six, each serving a specifically defined geographical district. In 1782 an additional treasurer's district was added. In 1784 the General Assembly eliminated the multiple districts and assigned the duties of the office to a single State Treasurer who was to be elected by a joint vote of both houses for a two-year term. This arrangement continued until 1868 when a new Constitution provided for the Treasurer to be elected by the people of North Carolina for a four-year term.

The longest serving Treasurer was John Haywood, who held the office for 40 years, from 1787 until his death in 1827. For much of his tenure, Treasurer Haywood dispensed funds from the "Publick Chest" kept in his office before there was ever a bank and even for years after the bank was established. William Sloan served just six weeks, at the end of the Civil War, and during that brief time, was accused of malfeasance. His accusers said he had stolen a warehouse full of cotton. John Stedman served 11 months in 1932, during the burgeoning days of the Great Depression. In this century Ben Lacy served the longest, 28 years. The average length of service has been eight years, not including of course, the situation of Robert H. Burton who was elected to the post but declined to serve a single day. John S. Haywood was elected Treasurer but declined to serve in the wake of an unfolding scandal involving missing funds from his father's tenure.

Only one State Treasurer, Jonathan Worth, a Whig, has ever been elected Governor, though many have aspired to become the State's chief executive. Worth had been a Whig in the 1840s and 1850s, but the party dissolved during the Civil War. Worth was a Conservative when he ran for Governor. The Conservatives became the reorganized Democratic Party during the mid-1870s. (Two district treasurers, Richard Caswell and Samuel Johnston served as Governor in the late 1700s.) One incumbent Treasurer, Charles M. Johnson, ran for Governor in 1948 as the favorite of the wing of the Democratic party in power then but lost in a spirited primary runoff election to W. Kerr Scott.

Without question, almost all of North Carolina's Treasurers have been honorable men who safeguarded the State's financial resources in an exemplary manner. In all of the 210 years of this office there have been fewer than a half dozen incidents of alleged malfeasance, and in only one of these was the amount of funds involved significant. In one case when a clerk was discovered embezzling funds in the Treasurer's office, he admitted the error of his deed, full restitution was made and the offender was hustled off to prison. In another case, the first singular Treasurer Memucan Hunt was accused of paying too generously soldiers who had fought in the Revolutionary War, and in some cases, paying soldiers who had not fought at all. The controversy arose as he was up for re-election and he lost to John Haywood. Haywood himself was accused of the most serious malfeasance but even in his case, though a substantial sum of public funds was lost, no personal dishonesty was ever proved against Haywood. Yet, the bulk of the missing money was repaid by Haywood's estate.

Four Treasurers died in office, four were defeated in re-election campaigns and four resigned from office. For many years, in fact until very recently, the Treasurer's position was an obscure post, since the State's budget was so small. Now, with annual budgets exceeding $17 billion and trust funds under management of some $30 billion, the work that the Treasurer and his staff does to account for and manage public funds is one of the most important duties in the State. Here is a brief account of the men who have served as the keeper of North Carolina's public purse for the past two centuries.

Table 3-1. Treasurers of North Carolina*

	Terms Began	Ended
Memucan Hunt	1784	1787
John Haywood	1787	1827
William S. Robards	1827	1830
William S. Mhoon	1830	1835
Samuel F. Patterson	1835	1837
Daniel W. Courts	1837	1839
Charles L. Hinton	1839	1843
John W. Wheeler	1843	1845
Charles L. Hinton	1845	1851
Daniel W. Courts	1851	1863
Jonathan Worth	1863	1865
Jonathan Worth (Provisional)	June 12, 1865	Nov. 16, 1865
William Sloan	Nov. 16, 1865	Jan. 1, 1866
Kemp P. Battle	Jan. 1, 1866	July 8, 1868
David A. Jenkins	July 8, 1868	Nov. 22, 1876
John M. Worth	Nov. 22, 1876	Jan. 21, 1885
Donald W. Bain	Jan. 21, 1885	Nov. 16, 1892
Samuel McDowell Tate	Nov. 16, 1892	Jan. 23, 1895
William H. Worth	Jan. 23, 1895	Jan. 15, 1901
Benjamin R. Lacy	Jan. 15, 1901	Feb. 23, 1929
Nathan O'Berry	Feb. 23, 1929	Jan. 7, 1932
John P. Stedman	Jan. 7, 1932	Nov. 21, 1932
Charles M. Johnson	Nov. 21, 1932	Jan. 6, 1949
Brandon P. Hodges	Jan. 6, 1949	July 20, 1953
Edwin M. Gill	July 20, 1953	Jan. 8, 1977
Harlan E. Boyles	Jan. 8, 1977	

*Note: There were a number of Treasurers appointed to serve the various districts within North Carolina between 1777 and 1784. The first singular Treasurer to be appointed to serve the entire state was Memucan Hunt and his term began in 1784.

Memucan Hunt
1784-1787

A native of Virginia, Memucan Hunt settled in Granville County (now Vance) on a plantation. At the age of 41, in 1770, Hunt was chosen Sergeant-at-Arms of the North Carolina General Assembly and in 1773 elected as Representative to the Assembly from Granville County. When the spirit of independence began to rise in the restless colony, Hunt represented Granville County in the five Provincial Congresses. In 1777, with the War for Independence underway, the fiscal needs of the colony were among its greatest concerns. Hunt was appointed Treasurer of the Hillsborough district, one of six district treasurers in the State at that time. He continued to hold office in the General Assembly and in 1779 was elected to the State Senate, serving as a member of the Committee of Accounts.

In November 1783, the General Assembly, in session at New Bern, abolished the district treasurer offices and established the singular fiscal position of State Treasurer and elected Hunt to fill the post. He took office on January 1, 1784, at a salary of 500 pounds per year.

During his term in office, Hunt unwittingly honored fraudulent claims for military service stemming from the Revolutionary War, which resulted in both litigation and hearings by the General Assembly. While he was not charged with malfeasance, he was not re-elected. Hunt retired from State politics to Granville County, where he became a wealthy planter and served as justice of the peace until 1792.

At the time of his death in 1808, at age 79, Hunt owned nearly 16,000 acres of land, 22 slaves, two horses, four mares, 14 head of cattle and 33 hogs.[4]

John Haywood
1787-1827

John Haywood served 40 years as Treasurer, far longer than any other person. At the time of his death, November 18, 1827, he was one of the most famous and beloved men in North Carolina, but that image would change soon. Haywood, a native of Edgecombe County, began public service in 1781 as clerk of the State Senate, a position he held five years, until elected Treasurer by the legislature.

When legislation was enacted requiring State officials to live in Raleigh, Haywood bought two choice lots (190 and 191) bounded by Person, Edenton, Blount and New Bern Streets where he built a house that stands today and is a popular meeting and entertainment place for small

[4]William S. Powell, *Dictionary of North Carolina Biography*, Vol. III (Chapel Hill: The University of North Carolina Press, 1988), 232.

groups. At this home, conveniently located adjacent to the Capitol, Haywood and his wife, Elizabeth, entertained official State visitors for many years. His wife, Eliza Eagles Asaph Williams, whom he married in 1798 after his first wife died, bore him 14 children.

After his death, a committee of the legislature examined Haywood's accounts and discovered that $68,906.80 was missing. That was a significant sum of money in 1827; in fact, it was more than half the State's entire budget that year. This news shocked the State's leading citizens who had come to know and respect Haywood as a great statesman. His estate reimbursed the State nearly $48,000, then a shortage totaling nearly $22,000 was discovered in the Cherokee bonds, involving sale of lands in western North Carolina. Haywood had been accused publicly of abusing his trust in 1820; however, an investigation by the legislature cleared him of wrongdoing.

According to historian William K. Boyd there were three defects in the accounting of public funds in those days.[5] "First the comptroller did not have oversight of the actual money in the treasury; the auditing by the comptroller did not include all State funds, and the method of bonding the Treasurer was not adequate." A 1784 law required that the Treasurer post a bond in the amount of 100,000 pounds. That law was changed in 1801 to require a bond equal to the balance of all funds in the treasury plus expected revenues for the next year, but there was no penalty for failing to provide security.

Haywood posted no bond for the years 1826-1827, so when the discrepancy was found in his accounts, the State was left short. Haywood's handling of the public funds was so haphazard that long after numerous banks were established, he continued to keep a trunk full of cash in the "Publick Chest" in his office which was used to pay the expenses of government. The accounting of these cash funds was notoriously inadequate by today's procedures. The State sued Haywood's estate for the missing funds; however, a jury found that an executor had administered all but $7,160.60 of the estate's assets which were then seized by judgment in favor of the State. In the end, most of Haywood's personal assets, except for a meager widow's dower rights, were seized by the State to settle the shortage of his account and his children were left with nothing.

Many citizens believed that the shortage was not Haywood's fault and

[5]William K. Boyd, *History of North Carolina*, Vol. II, *The Federal Period 1783-1860* (Chicago and New York: The Lewis Publishing Company, 1919), 109-113.

that he was not guilty of any major wrongdoing but, rather, was a poor bookkeeper. Scholars are still searching today for the answer to what happened to the funds which disappeared during his term in office. Haywood County, formed in 1808, was named for John Haywood.

John S. Haywood
declined to serve

John S. Haywood, son of the previous Treasurer, was elected to succeed his famous father, but in the wake of the unfolding scandal about missing funds from his father's tenure, young Haywood, wisely chose not to accept the post.

William S. Robards
1827-1830

Not much is known about William Robards who succeeded John Haywood as Treasurer and faced the unhappy duty of presiding over an office clouded with much controversy while the shortages in the accounts of his predecessor were uncovered. He was a member of the General Assembly in 1806 and 1808, representing Granville County where he also served as County Attorney. Following his single term as Treasurer, at the end of which he declined to run for reelection, Robards served for many years as clerk of the North Carolina Supreme Court. He was a close personal friend of U.S. Senator Willie P. Mangum.

Robert H. Burton
Elected in 1830, but declined to serve

Robert H. Burton was an enigma. Another native of Granville County, he moved to Lincoln County, began a successful law practice and became one of the county's leading citizens. In 1818, he was appointed a Judge of the Superior Court but after riding the circuit one term, he resigned.[6]

He was elected Treasurer by the legislature by a majority of eight votes over William Mhoon. Burton received 100 votes to Mhoon's 92. He had been recommended by Governor William A. Graham who became so angered with Burton's spurning the job that he wrote, "I saw Treasurer Burton at Lincoln County Court, and although I never felt colder weather,

[6]John W. Wheeler, *Historical Sketches of North Carolina from 1584-1851* (Philadelphia: Lippincott, Grambo & Co, 1851), 246.

he was in Court all week arguing six penny cases. He is so fond of money that I believe his conscience would take the cramp on a sixpence. As last Session of the Legislature was Resolution Session, they ought to have passed one more: 'Resolved that Rob Burton be compelled to wear a Petty-coat and bed gown the residue of his life and that said garments be made up out of the ragged treasury Bills instead of burning them,'—he is politically dead and d—d too."[7]

William S. Mhoon
1830-1835

William Spivey Mhoon was elected Treasurer by the legislature on December 20, 1830 when Robert H. Burton refused to serve. Mhoon served two, two-year terms, and he, too, declined to run for reelection. He had represented Bertie County in the House of Commons in 1828, 1829, 1830 and 1831. Between 1825 and 1835 he served at the University of North Carolina on the Committee of Appointments to Manage the Western Lands. Also he was appointed as one of the initial commissioners to supervise the rebuilding of the State Capitol on Union Square in 1832.[8]

Samuel F. Patterson
1835-1837

Samuel Finley Patterson was known for much of his life as General Patterson because of his previous appointments, first as brigadier of the militia and then as major general of the State militia, by the General Assembly during the Civil War. His two years as Treasurer were a small portion of his half century of public service.

Patterson's public career began at age 22 when he was elected engrossing clerk of the House of Commons. For the next 14 years he served in some capacity of clerkship in the legislature until 1834 when he was chosen chief clerk of the Senate. Later that same year he was elected by the legislature as State Treasurer. His popularity among the members of the General Assembly is somewhat hard to understand because a majority of the legislature at that time were supportive of the policies of Presi-

[7]J. G. deRoulhac Hamilton, ed., *Papers of William A. Graham*, Vol. I (Raleigh: State Department of Archives and History, 1957), 199.

[8]Jerry L. Cross, "Biographical Sketches of Seven State Treasurers" (Raleigh: North Carolina Department of Cultural Resources, 1994), 1.

dent Andrew Jackson, while Patterson was an outspoken and vocal opponent of Jackson. During part of the time he was Treasurer, Patterson also acted as president of the State Bank of North Carolina and acquired the reputation as one of the best financiers in North Carolina.

Patterson resigned as Treasurer abruptly in 1837 and returned to his business in Wilkesboro. In 1840 he was elected president of the Raleigh and Gaston Railroad, a position he held five years. He was elected to the Senate in 1846 and 1848, and in the Senate, became a leading advocate of a program of internal improvements focusing primarily upon the need to expand and improve the State's burgeoning railway system.

In 1854, he served his county in the House of Commons and, in 1864 was elected for the third time to the Senate. In 1868, he was nominated for the newly created post of Commissioner of Public Works as a member of the Conservative Party which went down to a smashing defeat. This was the only elective loss by Patterson during his long career. Among other positions he held were: Clerk of Superior Court, Clerk and Master in Equity and Indian Commissioner.

Historian Samuel A. Ashe was deeply impressed with the long and varied public career of veteran public servant Samuel Patterson. "What man in the State has ever lived a busier, more useful, purer life? Who, having so many and great trusts confided in him, has fulfilled them more worthily? He never sought any civil office which would withdraw him from North Carolina. His history, together with the history of a few of his peers and associates, was for many years the history of the State. Such men, so strong in mind and body, so pure in heart and hand, so steady, so resolute and so wise, during a half century of usefulness, influenced insensibly to themselves thousands whom they met and thousands more who honored them because of their acts," wrote Samuel Ashe.[9]

Daniel W. Courts
1837-1839
1851-1863

A native of Culpepper County, Virginia, Daniel Courts lived first in Rockingham County and then moved to Surry County, which he represented in the House of Commons from 1831 to 1833 and 1836. During his last term in the legislature, he was elected State Treasurer. He re-

[9]Samuel Ashe, Stephen B. Weeks, Charles L. Van Noppen, eds., *Biographical History of North Carolina from Colonial Times to the Present*, Vol. II (Greensboro: Charles L. Van Noppen Publisher, 1905-1917), 328-333.

signed as Treasurer in 1839, after serving only two years, to accept an appointment by President Martin Van Buren as the U.S. Consul at Matanza, Cuba. He stayed in Cuba briefly and returned to North Carolina, settling in Rockingham County which he represented in the House of Commons in 1846 and 1848 and in the Senate in 1850.

In 1851, he was again elected State Treasurer and this time he served ably until 1863. When North Carolina seceded from the Union, Courts was a member of the faction of the Democratic party which strongly supported secession. He was defeated for re-election in 1862 by Jonathan Worth.

In 1864, Courts was again elected to represent Rockingham County in the Senate. In his prime, Courts was a wealthy plantation owner, holding title to more than a thousand acres in Rockingham County and 40 slaves. During the chaos following the Civil War, Courts, like many of his peers, was forced to sell his property to pay his debts. He died in Raleigh in 1883 at the age of 83.

Charles L. Hinton

1839-1843
1845-1851

Charles Lewis Hinton was a major of the militia, planter, legislator and, in 1839, became State Treasurer. Hinton represented his native Wake County in both the House of Commons and the Senate. He also was a member of the commissions for rebuilding the State Capitol and for building the State Hospital for the Insane. He served as Treasurer for 11 years in two different terms. He also served as a commissioner for sale of the Indian lands and was a trustee of the University of North Carolina for 28 years.

He was born at the Oaks Plantation in Wake County where he was buried in 1861.

Jonathan Worth

1863-1865
(Provisional) June 12 - November 16, 1865

Jonathan Worth, native of Guilford County, settled in Randolph County and made his fame and fortune there as an attorney and legislator. A Quaker and protege of Judge Archibald Murphey, Worth championed the cause of free public schools during his tenure in the legislature and, though he belonged to the greatly outnumbered Whig party, gained much stature for the practical nature of his ideas and the respect for his vision for improving North Carolina.

In 1830, he ran for a seat in the legislature from Randolph County, motivated in large part by a failing law practice. His major shortcoming, he had decided, was his deficiency as a public speaker. His peers at the Bar persuaded him there was no better way to improve his oratory and achieve better rhetoric than to become a member of the North Carolina General Assembly which thrives on talk.

He served two terms in the House, took a break from public service to build a lucrative law practice, was elected to the State Senate and then ran twice for Congress, both times unsuccessfully.

In 1858, Worth found himself back in the State Senate where he was made chairman of a committee to investigate the poorly run North Carolina Railroad. He pursued this official duty so relentlessly that the president of the Railroad, formerly a good friend, challenged Worth to a duel which he wisely declined.

Worth was an avid opponent of North Carolina's secession from the Union. Though opposed to the Confederate stands on most issues, Worth remained loyal to North Carolina's cause and refused to take part in several peace movements. He was elected State Treasurer by acclamation by the legislature.

Worth had the unhappy duty of issuing notes and bonds to finance the State's share of its war debt. Of the some $20 million in notes authorized by the State, Worth issued $8.5 million and $5.2 million were outstanding at the end of the war. War bonds totaling more than $13 million were issued. At the end of the war, all of the State's war debt was repudiated. Worth was considered a good Treasurer, doing the best he could to safeguard the financial resources of the people of North Carolina during troubled times.

Just before Raleigh was occupied by Sherman's conquering forces at the end of the war, Governor Zebulon Vance charged Worth with the duty of safeguarding the State archives which he did by evacuating them to the Company Shops in Alamance County. Worth was so highly regarded that when William W. Holden was installed as the provisional Governor, he requested Worth be named the provisional Treasurer, a title Worth held for five months until he was elected Governor. Worth is the only statewide Treasurer to become Governor.[10]

[10]Ashe, Week, Van Noppen, *Biographical History*, Vol. III, 454-460.

William Sloan

November 16, 1865 - Jan 1, 1866

William Sloan served the briefest term of any State Treasurer. He was appointed by provisional Governor William W. Holden and held office until elected officials took office January 1, 1866. He served as a delegate to the Constitutional Convention of 1865-1866 and was chairman of the Convention's redistricting committee.

As Treasurer, Sloan was accused of selling a large quantity of the State's cotton to a business partner at prices well below market value. Opponents accused him of attempting to defraud the State of $500, a large sum of money at that time.

Following his brief term as Treasurer, Sloan became president of the Wilmington, Charlotte and Rutherford Railroad and was implicated in the widespread railroad bond frauds, which occurred during the Reconstruction Period.[11]

Kemp P. Battle

January 1, 1866 - July 8, 1868

Kemp Plummer Battle is known more widely for his association with the University of North Carolina than for his two-year tenure as State Treasurer. Battle graduated from the University in 1849 as the valedictorian of his class. During the next five years he worked at the university, as tutor of Latin and then as tutor of mathematics, while studying law under the tutelage of his father. He was admitted to the Bar in 1854 and began a practice in Raleigh. In 1857, he was named a director of the rechartered Bank of North Carolina and in 1861 was a delegate to the Secession Convention. During the Civil War he served as president of the Chatham Railroad which existed primarily to haul coal from the mines in Chatham County to Confederate armament factories.

In 1862, Battle was elected by the legislature to serve as trustee of the University and held this position until 1868, when the entire board was thrown out by the Reconstruction General Assembly. He was elected Treasurer by the legislature in 1866 but removed from office in 1868 by the occupying U.S. military authorities because of his service to the Confederacy.

In 1874, Battle was reappointed a trustee to the University, a position he served for the rest of his life. He was named president of the Univer-

[11]Cross, "Biographical Sketches," 1.

sity in 1876 and served ably until 1891, when he resigned to become Alumni Professor of History. He became a distinguished historian and compiled a significant body of scholarly work, the most prominent piece being his two-volume History of the University of North Carolina which is still today considered a significant study.[12]

David A. Jenkins

July 8, 1868 - November 22, 1876

After serving two years in the General Assembly, Jenkins ran in the general election of 1868 as the Republican candidate for State Treasurer and became the first State Treasurer elected statewide. Reflecting his astuteness as a politician, he immediately employed his predecessor and his opponent, Kemp Battle, as an advisor. He hired another Democrat, Donald Bain, as chief clerk. Bain would become Treasurer himself in a decade.

Jenkins served as North Carolina's Treasurer during a time of great despair. The Civil War had taken the lives of 40,000 of the State's best men and thousands of others returned home minus an arm, an eye, a leg, or maimed in yet another serious way. More than $200 million of the State's wealth had been wiped out with the abolition of slavery.[13]

All of North Carolina's surplus funds had been consumed by the war. Some $10 million in Confederate taxes, according to historian Hugh T. Lefler, had been consumed in the losing cause. The war left North Carolina with many of its best young men dead, its treasury empty and its government in shambles.

Jenkins was re-elected in 1872. His tenure as Treasurer coincided with one of the stormiest and most scandal-ridden periods in the State's history. During Reconstruction, North Carolina was governed by a Republican coalition of former union sympathizers, native blacks and "carpetbaggers." The "carpetbaggers" were mostly Yankees who came South after the war, carrying all their earthly belongings in carpetbags, thus their unaffectionate nickname. It was during this time the greatest financial scandal in the history of the State occurred. The Republican legislatures of 1868 and 1869 issued a total of $27.8 million in railroad bonds which were discovered to be embroiled in widespread fraud. Railroad officials had given or "loaned" more than a quarter of a million dollars to

[12]Powell, *Dictionary*, 114-115.

[13]Hugh Talmage Lefler and Albert Ray Newsome, *The History of a Southern State, North Carolina* (Chapel Hill: The University of North Carolina Press, 1963), 448.

key legislators in exchange for their support in issuing the bonds. Huge sums from the bond proceeds went into the pockets of lawyers, legislators, top railroad officials and even one judge was accused of accepting a payoff.[14]

When Democrats regained control of the General Assembly one of their first acts was to repudiate the fraudulent railroad bonds. Although neither Treasurer Jenkins nor Governor W. W. Holden was personally implicated in the scandal or charged with receiving any of the stolen proceeds, they would have had to be naive not to know what was going on around them. Jenkins was regarded as honest and respectable by his contemporaries, and his opponents; however, he resigned before the end of his last term.[15]

John M. Worth

November 22, 1876 - January 21, 1885

John Milton Worth was the younger brother of Jonathan Worth who served as Treasurer and Governor during the 1860s. John Worth served several terms in the State Senate, representing Moore and Montgomery Counties in the 1840s. Like his older brother, he was a Unionist or Anti-Secessionist, until the war broke out and then he became loyal to the southern cause, serving as commanding officer of the Sixth Reserves.

In 1870, he was elected Senator from Randolph County. It was not a good time for the State. The Republican legislature of 1868 had looted the State treasury, authorizing some $16 million in bonds (later found to be fraudulent and repudiated) on top of previous debt equal to that sum, and Governor W. W. Holden had been impeached by the General Assembly and removed from office.

When David Jenkins resigned before the end of his term, Governor Brogden named Worth to fill the unexpired term as Treasurer. He already had been elected to serve a four-year term in November. His name added strength to the ticket and is credited with helping the Democrats regain power in the State. As Treasurer, he faced up to the difficult task of settling the State's debt on a fair and equitable basis to both the bond holders and the citizens of the State.

Worth was re-elected Treasurer in 1880, serving just over four more years. He served the State well, with honor, integrity and capability and was highly respected for his service. He is quoted as once commenting

[14]Lefler and Newsome, *The History of a Southern State*, 465.
[15]Powell, *Dictionary*, Vol. III, 227.

upon his guiding philosophy, saying, "My earnest wish has been to be useful to the State."

After leaving public service, Worth became president of the Bank of Randolph and of the Southern Stock Mutual Fire Insurance Company. His Worth Manufacturing Company operated successful cotton mills in Worthville and Central Falls in Randolph County, not far from where the North Carolina Zoological Park is located today. By the time of his death in 1900 at age 90, he had become one of the State's wealthiest citizens.[16]

Donald W. Bain

January 21, 1885 - November 16, 1892

Donald Bain, a native of Raleigh, might be called North Carolina's first finance professional to occupy the office of State Treasurer. He began a 35-year career in State service as the youngest clerk in the State Controller's office while he was still in his teens. In 1865, he accepted an appointment as chief clerk of the State Treasurer's office, a post he held almost 20 years.

Bain was elected Treasurer in 1884 and served from 1885 until his death in 1892. Bain was an honest, conscientious and devoted public servant. He was re-elected in the November 1892, general election to a third term but died nine days after the election.[17]

Samuel McDowell Tate

November 16, 1892 - January 23, 1895

Colonel Samuel McDowell Tate, veteran of the Civil War, helped organize a company from his native Burke County and fought gallantly as part of that famous defense at Manassas Junction where General Thomas Jackson became known simply as "Stonewall." Tate fought at Richmond, at Second Manassas, at Sharpsburg, at Gettysburg, and at Rappahannock. He was wounded just as the war was ending.

After the war he was elected president of the bankrupt Western North Carolina Railroad. Tate was forced out of office by the Reconstruction Acts, because of his war record, by Governor W. W. Holden. He was elected to the legislature in 1874 and served subsequent terms in the House in 1881, 1883 and 1885. In 1886, he was appointed federal examiner of

[16]Ashe, Weeks and Van Noppen, *Biographical History*, Vol. III, 454-460.
[17]Powell, *Dictionary*, 86.

National Banks for the district stretching from West Virginia to Florida.

Upon the death of Donald Bain, Governor Thomas M. Holt appointed Colonel Tate, his longtime friend, as State Treasurer. The record shows he served briefly but ably. He was nominated by the Democratic Party to succeed himself in 1894; however, the fusion of Populists and Republicans into a common ticket defeated the Democrats for many statewide offices that year in what became known as the Fusion campaign. Colonel Tate retired to his home in Burke County where he died two years later.[18]

William H. Worth

January 23, 1895 - January 15, 1901

The third member of the Worth family of Randolph County to serve as Treasurer, William Henry Worth was a devout Quaker. Having taken no role in the Civil War, Worth was not among the white males who failed to qualify for public office during Reconstruction. He served as Assessor of Internal Revenue for the Third North Carolina District from 1866 to 1870 and then settled on a farm near Kinston in Lenoir County. After he made a name for himself as business agent for Lenoir County, he was appointed State business agent in 1889, serving in that position until December 31, 1894.

During the Fusion campaign of 1894, Worth was nominated as the Populist Party's candidate for Treasurer to oppose Colonel Samuel McDowell Tate for the remaining two years of the unexpired term of Donald Bain who had died in office. After defeating Tate, Worth was re-elected for a full term in 1896. Though Worth himself was a person of integrity, the embezzlement of $16,000 by a veteran clerk was discovered by Worth's successor. Worth, at considerable personal sacrifice, covered the loss so that neither the State nor the bondsman suffered any loss. Historian Samuel Ashe was highly impressed with Worth's diligence to make the matter right. "By this act of honor and self-sacrifice neither the State nor any of the Treasurer's bondsmen were losers, though the result of years of toil was thereby swept from the possession of Mr. Worth to make good the shortage of another," wrote Ashe.[19]

[18]Ashe, Weeks and Van Noppen, *Biographical History*, 430-439.
[19]Ashe, Weeks and Van Noppen, *Biographical History*, 480.

Benjamin R. Lacy

January 15, 1901 - February 21, 1929

Benjamin Rice Lacy served 28 years as State Treasurer, longer than anyone else in this century, and he did so with great honor and distinction. In his first Treasurer's report, Lacy detailed how he discovered the embezzlement that had occurred during the previous several years.

"When I was installed in this office, I retained the clerks who had served under my predecessor until my appointees were sufficiently familiar with their duties to perform them with ease and accuracy," Lacy wrote in his December 15, 1902 report.

"It is fortunate for the State that I did in this instance, for it resulted in the early discovery of a systematic fraud which had been practiced for five years, and the recovery of $16,060.04 for the State. The State's money was obtained by Major Martin, Institutional Clerk, by altering checks passing through his hands and making corresponding forced balances in his books. The first altered check he attempted to use under the new administration resulted in the detection of the fraud, his confession of guilt, conviction and sentence to the State's Prison for ten years."

During the last eight years of his term, North Carolina launched an unprecedented program of expansion in which the Treasurer's office handled millions of dollars. Lacy's office managed the financing of $50 million in road construction, approved by State voters in 1921. In addition to that, nearly $20 million of school construction occurred during this period.[20]

Though Lacy never graduated from college, he was awarded an honorary doctorate of laws degree by Davidson College in 1928 where his father, a Presbyterian pastor for 18 years, had served as president during the 1850s.

Lacy was a "railroad man" for many years, working as an apprentice in the shops of the Raleigh and Gaston Railroad at Raleigh, where he became a foreman and for fifteen years ran a locomotive. He was known for his fairness and his special concern for the working man. After serving as an Alderman for the City of Raleigh, he became commissioner of labor and printing in 1894.

He died just one month after being sworn in for his eighth term.

[20]Lefler and Newsome, *The History of a Southern State*, 566-568.

Nathan O'Berry

February 23, 1929 - January 6, 1932

Nathan O'Berry was appointed by Governor O. Max Gardner to fill the unexpired term of Ben Lacy. He, too, died in office before having the opportunity to seek reelection. O'Berry was a successful businessman, having made a fortune in the lumber business before his appointment to the Commission for the State Hospital for Colored Insane in Goldsboro. He served as chairman of this Commission from 1925 until 1929 and his achievements were so significant that a new building there, the O'Berry Center, and subsequently the entire complex, was named for him. He also served on the Advisory Committee for the Caswell Training Center and in 1926 was appointed to the State Educational Commission.[21]

John P. Stedman

January 7, 1932 - November 21, 1932

No Treasurer ever faced grimmer circumstances than did John Porterfield Stedman, who though serving only 11 months, was known primarily as a "caretaker" of the office. During his brief tenure, Stedman faced one of the State's most challenging crises.

The really bad times of the Great Depression were drawing nigh in 1932. Banks were failing, real estate values were falling and revenue for both the State and numerous local governments was declining to the point that many public entities were in default of their financial obligations. At the time of his appointment as Treasurer, Stedman was 37 years old and one of the youngest men ever to hold the position.

Following his brief term as Treasurer–he did not seek election to a full term–he worked for a number of banks and in 1939 became president of the Scottish Bank in Lumberton, a position he held for several years. He was president of the North Carolina Bankers Association from 1953 to 1954. Stedman was appointed by Governor Luther Hodges to the State Banking Commission in 1957 and served until 1963. He died in 1973 at age 80.[22]

[21]Boyd, *History of North Carolina*, Vol.5, 269.
[22]Cross, "Biographical Sketches," 2.

Charles M. Johnson

November 21, 1932 - January 6, 1949

Charles Marion Johnson came to the office of Treasurer, well-experienced and already seasoned in the area of public finance. Prior to his appointment in 1932, Johnson had served as deputy clerk of court of Pender County for seven years and then 18 months as district tax supervisor under the Revaluation Act. Then he worked five years in various capacities in the State Auditor's office, serving first as a traveling auditor, one year as auditor of disbursements, and finally as deputy auditor.

He was appointed secretary to the County Government Advisory Commission by Governor Angus W. McLean and in this position became familiar with the concerns of local governments throughout North Carolina, as they were entering a period of hard times. His success in this position, particularly his ability to deal with county leaders in an honest and frank manner, led Governor O. Max Gardner to appoint him as the first Secretary of the Local Government Commission, which was created by the General Assembly in 1931. Johnson's great sense of humor, no doubt, helped him succeed during these times.

Shortly before the end of Governor Gardner's administration, Johnson was named Treasurer. In 1933, Governor J. C. B. Ehringhaus recommended, and the General Assembly concurred, that the Local Government Commission be consolidated in the Treasurer's office, where it remains today.

Johnson served North Carolina ably during the Great Depression. He became a highly trusted and respected financial advisor not only to the several Governors who served during the decade of despair, but he also assisted county and city leaders with their financial and budgetary difficulties. As Treasurer, Johnson gained the trust of New York bond investors. Because of their confidence in the ability of the State and its local governments to recover, Johnson persuaded bond investors to negotiate re-payment schedules until the State and the nation saw better economic times.

Johnson was re-elected to successive terms until 1948 when he became a candidate for Governor and was favored by the faction of the Democratic Party that had ruled North Carolina for several decades. He led the primary by a small margin, but was forced into a runoff by W. Kerr Scott, formerly the Commissioner of Agriculture. Scott won the primary runoff and the general election in November, campaigning on the promise to get farmers out of the mud by improving the State's farm-to-market roads. Johnson was criticized during the campaign for allowing the State's surplus funds to sit idle in banks and not earn interest that should be accruing for the benefit of taxpayers. Johnson never harbored bitterness because of his defeat, but became active and successful in both private and public ventures.

He joined First Securities Corporation in Durham and later became executive vice president of the Bank of Charlotte. He was appointed by President Harry Truman as Collector of Customs at Wilmington. He was appointed by Governor Terry Sanford to the State Banking Commission where he served two terms.[23]

Brandon P. Hodges

January 6, 1949 - July 20, 1953

Brandon Hodges, an attorney from Buncombe County, represented the 31st District in the State Senate from 1943 to 1945. He was chairman of the Senate Appropriations Committee in 1945 and a member of the Advisory Budget Commission the following year. In 1947, Governor Gregg Cherry named Hodges his executive general counsel. He served as chairman of the Board of Trustees of Western Carolina Teachers College and also as a member of the State Education Commission 1947-1948.

In 1948, he became the Democratic nominee for Treasurer, was elected in November and took office January 6, 1949. Hodges was reelected in 1952, but resigned just six months into his second term to return to private business. He became counsel to Champion Paper and Fibre Company. In 1955 Governor Luther Hodges (no relation) appointed Brandon Hodges to serve as chairman of the State's first modern day Tax Study Commission and in 1957 he was named chairman of the State Property Tax Commission.[24]

Edwin Maurice Gill

July 20, 1953 - January 8, 1977

Mr. Edwin Gill was my friend and mentor. I knew him for 30 years and during that time came to know him as one of North Carolina's greatest public servants. A native of Laurinburg, he entered Trinity College in 1922 and left two years later, after passing the Bar examination. While

[23]Powell, *Dictionary*, 287.
[24]Cross, "Biographical Sketches," 2.

practicing law in Scotland County, he was elected to represent the County in the 1929 and 1931 sessions of the General Assembly.

In the legislature, he was a member of the subcommittees which drafted legislation creating the Local Government Commission and the takeover by the State of county road construction and maintenance.

When the 1931 General Assembly adjourned, Governor O. Max Gardner named Gill as his private secretary. In 1933, Governor J. C. B. Ehringhaus appointed Gill to head the newly created North Carolina Paroles Commission, a position he held 11 years. In 1942 he was appointed Commissioner of Revenue by Governor J. Melville Broughton, serving in that position seven years.

In 1949 Gill joined former Governor Gardner in a Washington, D.C. law firm but left a year later to accept the appointment by President Harry Truman as collector of internal revenue for North Carolina.

In 1953, Gill was appointed State Treasurer by Governor William B. Umstead, to fill the unexpired term of Brandon Hodges. He was reelected State Treasurer successfully until his retirement in 1977.

Mr. Gill, as everyone called him, was a brilliant man, well-read, and a lover of the arts. As a young man, he attended the New York School of Fine and Applied Arts. He painted as a hobby and was a zealous supporter of the North Carolina Art Museum. He was also a respectable pianist and organist.

His greatest asset was his impeccable personal integrity and his great devotion to North Carolina. A lifelong bachelor, he considered the State and all its inhabitants his personal concern. On many a Saturday morning, Mr. Gill would call me and suggest we ought to go to the office and conduct the public's business. Inevitably, I would find myself on Saturday mornings driving to the Sir Walter Hotel where he lived and taking him to the office for a few hours work. I believe he felt guilty about being away from the office any time there was work to be done. He answered the telephone himself.

Mr. Gill's greatest achievement as State Treasurer was North Carolina's attaining its Triple-A credit rating in the early 1960s, which we have maintained continuously since. That feat has saved taxpayers millions of dollars in bond interest payments and has been a source of great pride among business and financial leaders. At a time when the national government and many other state governments have become careless with public funds entrusted to them, North Carolina citizens have benefitted immensely from the example of financial prudence set into place by Edwin Gill.

Governor Dan K. Moore, commenting on Mr. Gill's financial acumen, once said, "Ed Gill is the only man I know who can see around a corner."

He is credited with coining the phrase, "In North Carolina, we have made a habit of good government," and he came to be known, as "Mr. Integrity."

Mr. Gill left big shoes to fill in the office of State Treasurer and his example is an ideal one to emulate.

During his years in Raleigh he was a member of the Edenton Street Methodist Church, where he taught Sunday School. Both Duke University and Campbell College awarded him honorary degrees. He died in July 1978 and was buried in Hillside Cemetery in Laurinburg.

Harlan Edward Boyles

January 8, 1977 -

I learned from my father, in the dark moments of the Great Depression, a lesson in basic economics which has guided my management of the State's money to this day.

Whenever I would go down to the little store my father ran in Lincoln County to get a soft drink, my father would tell me we had to sell roughly three loaves of bread to make up for what that drink cost. My father explained that the drink cost five cents and we made two cents on each loaf of bread. I learned then to equate the benefits of something with its cost.

Before becoming State Treasurer in 1977, I served as Deputy Treasurer for 16 years, second in command to the late Edwin Gill, an able and innovative leader who was one of North Carolina's most devoted public servants. Before that, I was a tax auditor in the North Carolina Department of Revenue, and later a staff adviser to the N.C. Tax Study Commission, which laid the foundation for improving this State's business climate.

There are two important achievements of my tenure as Treasurer of which I am proud. The first is our ability in North Carolina to maintain the Triple-A credit rating which was obtained during the leadership of my predecessor in 1960. We talk much about the importance of North Carolina's maintaining its Triple-A credit rating and it is a very significant thing for our taxpayers. It translates directly in the savings of millions of dollars for them each year.

North Carolina's retention of its Triple-A credit rating, even during difficult times when the State faced major budget crises, is a singular fiscal achievement and one that we should always safeguard. North Carolina is one of only four states which have a Triple-A credit rating. Nine local government units in North Carolina also have a Triple-A credit rating and this is the highest number of any state, representing 25 percent of all Triple-A credit rated local governments in the nation.

Second, I am proud of the modernization techniques we have employed in the Treasurer's Office over the years. Our office has been at the leading edge of putting new technology to work, beginning with electronic deposits and continuing with the advanced use of computers to take advantage of every opportunity for increased efficiency. Our office has one of the most important jobs in all of North Carolina State government, yet we do that job with a small workforce–and we do the job well.

The North Carolina Treasurer's Office has one of the most aggressive Escheat and Unclaimed Property programs in the nation. Through this program thousands of citizens are found and notified each year of unclaimed property which belongs to them. In 1993, some 2,300 students received loans to attend public institutions of higher learning, from the $6.7 million in interest earnings from the Escheat and Unclaimed Property funds.

The State budget has increased from $3 billion to nearly $17 billion during my tenure as State Treasurer. During the same time the State workforce has grown from 158,000 to 218,000. And the total trust funds under management by the Treasurer have grown from $3.6 billion in 1976 to nearly $31 billion in 1994. By the end of this century the State's trust funds are projected to comprise a $50 billion portfolio.

Personal

I was born May 6, 1929, in Lincoln County, and have been married 42 years to the former Frankie Wilder of Johnston County. We have two daughters and one son. I graduated from the University of North Carolina in 1951 with a degree in accounting and became a Certified Public Accountant in 1955.

I have served as president of the National Association of State Auditors, Comptrollers and Treasurers; president of the Raleigh Rotary Club; chairman of the Wake County Salvation Army Advisory Board; member of the North Carolina Association of Certified Public Accountants; member of the U.S. Securities and Exchange Commission's Municipal Securities Rulemaking Board, member of the North Carolina Art Society; member of the John Motley Morehead Memorial Commission; president of the Raleigh Executive's Club; deacon, elder, treasurer and clerk of the Westminster Presbyterian Church; and long have been active in the Democratic party.

The Treasurer serves as an ex-officio member of the Council of State; Chairman, Local Government Commission; Chairman, Tax Review Board; Chairman, State Banking Commission; Chairman, Board of Trustees, Teachers' and State Employees Retirement System; Chairman, Board of Trustees, Local Governmental Employees' Retirement System; Chairman, Firemen's and Rescue Workers' Pension Fund; Member, State Board of Education; Member, State Board of Community Colleges; Member, Capital Planning Commission; Member, North Carolina Housing Commission; Member, North Carolina Global TransPark Authority.

Chapter 4

Taxes: Where Do They Come From?

Inflation is the friend of the tax collector and the enemy of the taxpayer because inflation increases the amount of money while decreasing its value. The result of inflation is a false sense of prosperity–more money for the office holders and a reduced standard of living for most people.

Taxes have been both the bane and blessing of civilized society since the advent of recorded history. With the good and prudent use of taxes, mankind has been able to conquer new frontiers, combat tyranny, cure disease, abolish ignorance, and create comfort where hardship once existed.

Taxes, as they have increased sharply in recent years, have come to play an increasingly important role in the lives of everyone.

When Professor Raymond T. Bye wrote, in 1924, his respected college textbook on economics, entitled Principles of Economics, the subject of taxes came up only once, only on one page and then only in a minor discussion of how to determine the basic costs of goods and services.[25] That was because in Professor Bye's pre-Great Depression Days, taxes were so low at both the federal and state levels as to be considered an insignificant cost of doing business.

Now, turn to any economics textbook and you will find the subject of taxes has assumed a major, if not decisive, role in economic planning. In their 1987 college textbook entitled, Economics, Professors Richard G. Lipsey, Peter O. Steiner and Douglas D. Purvis devote an entire chapter, totalling some 25 pages, to the subject of "Taxation and Public Expenditure." They conclude: "Government spending and government taxation today go far beyond the minimum required to provide such essentials as a system of justice and protection against foreign enemies. Spending and taxing are also key tools of both macroeconomic and microeconomic policy."[26]

[25]Raymond T. Bye, *Principles of Economics* (New York: F. S. Crofts & Company, 1924), 330.

[26]Richard G. Lipsey, Peter O. Steiner and Douglas D. Purvis, *Economics*, 8th ed. (New York: Harper & Row, Publishers, 1987), 431.

History of Taxes

The history of man is a history of taxation of private wealth to advance the public good. Scholars have discovered that before man learned to count, he learned to tax. In fact, there is historic evidence that the necessity for learning to count arose from the need by an early ruler to assure his loyal and faithful servants paid their lawful obligations to the kingdom. Ancient kings and emperors collected their assessments in grain, animals, furs, shells, silk, cloth, fruit, honey, salt, and other commodities long before the advent of money (in the form of copper, iron, gold, silver, and banknotes.) As the empires grew and expanded their control over other countries and other cultures, it became necessary to employ the services of a new breed of public servants called tax collectors, whose profession would become, if not the first, certainly the most maligned means of earning a livelihood. To make sure the first line collectors remained honest, others were hired to supervise, to check and double check records and accounts of the tax collectors to guard against graft, pilfering, bribery, embezzlement and other measures of attrition against the treasury. Hence the bureaucracy was born.

Historians have found structured systems of financial administration, with crude forms of levying and collecting taxes, dating back as far as ancient Egypt in the year 3100 B.C., more than 5,000 years ago.[27]

The initial purpose of the first taxes, most often collected in the form of food grains, was to provide food for the king and his household, to feed the king's army which defended his rule, and in rare cases of famine to provide food for the population in times of desperate need. Remember the famous Biblical story of Joseph, the favored son of Jacob who, with his coat of many colors, was sold into slavery in Egypt by his jealous brothers? Joseph rose because of his gift of interpreting dreams to become Governor of Egypt. When he interpreted Pharaoh's dream forewarning of seven fat years followed by seven years of famine, he wisely advised his ruler to collect enough surplus during the good years to sustain the people during their coming hard times. Joseph specifically advised the Pharaoh to take 20 percent of the harvest during the good seven years for use during the famine. It was one of the earliest examples of a good tax.

In today's sophisticated times, modern governments have adopted the philosophy of taxing constituents on their ability to pay. In ancient times,

[27]Carolyn Webber and Aaron Wildavsky, *A History of Taxation and Expenditure In the Western World* (New York: Simon and Schuster, 1986), 39.

governments appeared to levy taxes primarily upon the ability to make its subjects pay.

The Bible contains numerous references to the influence of taxes at the time Jesus walked the good earth. In fact, it was the issue of taxes which dictated the place of Jesus' birth, one of the most significant events in the history of mankind. "And it came to pass in those days, that there went out a decree from Caesar Augustus, that all the world should be taxed." Luke 2:1.

No doubt, it was their misery from the oppressive 42 percent tax rate which gave the children of Israel more than a heavenly reason to await the arrival of the Messiah and save them from the intolerant Romans.

The Old Testament is sprinkled with information about taxes. In the book of II Kings, there is the story of the Israelites who paid the king of Assyria handsomely to leave them alone. "And Pul the king of Assyria came against the land: and Menahem gave Pul a thousand talents of silver, that his hand might be with him to confirm the kingdom in his hand.

"And Menahem exacted the money of Israel, even of all the mighty men of wealth, of each man fifty shekels of silver, to give to the king of Assyria. So the king of Assyria turned back, and stayed not there in the land." II Kings 15:19-20.

The apostle Matthew, author of the first book in the New Testament and disciple of Christ, was himself a former tax collector, as was Zacchaeus, who at the time of his conversion was chief among the publicans (tax collectors) in the city of Jericho.

Wise rulers have been cautious in the confiscation of private wealth and its appropriation for the public good. The judicious use of public funds has unlocked the mysteries to fatal diseases, defended the province against tyranny and built the foundations of great societies. Excessive taxation and the misuse of public resources have unraveled the fabric of great cultures such as the Roman, Greek and Egyptian Empires. In almost every case of governmental extravagance, constituents grew weary of oppressive taxation and found innovative ways to avoid paying their legal share. It was at that point that the empires, one by one, in their own time began to crumble. Such were the circumstances which gave birth to our own republic just over two centuries ago.

Good Taxes

Good taxes, Adam Smith wrote in his 1776 book, *Wealth of Nations*, meet four criteria. First, they should be based on an individual's ability to pay. Second, good taxes should be certain. Third, they should be convenient to collect and fourth, they should be efficient and economical. For two centuries industrialized nations of the western world have generally followed these basic principles of Adam Smith. But in the past two decades, there are signs that several modern day governments, including our own in Washington and Raleigh, have strayed from the principles of fairness, certainty, convenience, and economy of scale.

North Carolina Taxes

North Carolina taxes generally have been fair, reasonable, convenient, and certain, in short meeting all the criteria which Adam Smith set out. Fresh memories of the oppressive actions by merciless British tax collectors served as a great inhibitor against loose tax policies of the new republic.

Local taxes were first authorized by the Colonial Assembly in 1722 for the singular purpose of building courthouses and jails. Under the highly centralized colonial form of government, counties existed to serve solely as agents of the colonial government and were created for the purpose of administering government services at the local level. Their power was limited to the specific authority granted by the colonial government, either the Lords Proprietor or the Colonial Assembly. The chief local administrator was the justice of peace who was appointed by the Governor upon the recommendation of the county's representatives in the Colonial Assembly.

Unlike northern colonies where the ad valorem property tax became an important source of revenue, property taxes remained low in North Carolina. This was so primarily because of the dominant influence in the Colonial Assembly, and later in the General Assembly after the Revolutionary War, by wealthy eastern North Carolina landowners whose best interests were served by low property taxes. Instead, the poll, or head tax, became a major revenue generator. In 1812 the poll tax yielded twice as much revenue as the land tax and was still the State's largest source of revenue at the beginning of the Civil War.[28]

Total State expenditures per capita increased fivefold, from $0.23 in 1836 to $1.24 in 1860.[29] One of the reasons for rising taxes during this period was the necessity for paying for the beautiful new Capitol. In

[28]Charles D. Liner, "The Origins and Development of the North Carolina Tax System of Taxation," *Popular Government*, 45(Summer 1979): 41-49.

[29]Liner, "The Origins and Development," 43.

1840, when the State Capitol was built at what then was considered the exorbitant cost of $540,000, that sum represented more than two complete years of tax revenue.

Taxation Begins

Between the American Revolution and the Civil War, every initiative to add new taxes or increase existing levies was greeted with great resistance. North Carolina's revenue came chiefly from the poll tax, a nominal property tax and a variety of license taxes through the 19th Century. The State's first income tax was enacted in 1849; however, it applied only to the interest, dividends and some profits received by persons of wealth. The State income tax as we know it today was enacted in 1921 and applicable to the net proceeds of all kinds of income. The first broad income tax was palatable to the general public because it applied to so few of the people. The initial rate of one percent applied to the first $2,500 of income, but provided for a $1,000 exemption for a single individual and a $2,000 exemption for married couples, plus an additional $200 exemption for each child. The maximum income tax rate of three percent applied only to those very few and fortunate persons earning more than $10,000 per year. In 1921, the per capita income in North Carolina was less than $300, which meant that only the very wealthy had to pay any personal income tax at all.

Having gotten their hand into the taxpayer's wallet, North Carolina lawmakers lost no time raising the ante. The rate was increased in 1925 and again in 1931 and 1933 by which time the original rate had been doubled. In 1937, the North Carolina income tax rate was increased substantially again, to the levels which have remained essentially the same today–except for constant tinkering to spread the net to gather a wider catch–three percent for the first $2,000; four percent for the next $2,000; five percent for the next $2,000; six percent for the next $4,000; and seven percent for income over $10,000.

It did not make much sense to tax income prior to 1900 because there was little cash income earned by the preponderance of small farmers who toiled the soil from daylight to dark, clearing the virgin forests, planting their tracts, and earning their meager subsistence from the land itself. The farmer planted his crop in the spring, taking seed from the best of his harvest for another crop and feeding his family through the winter on what he could store. Fish from the ocean and the backwoods rivers as well as game from the wilderness provided ample protein and recreation.

It was a Spartan existence and one which offered few temptations for the tax collector.

In 1800, the State budget was less than $50,000 and came primarily from an individual poll tax, property taxes and land sales. At the time of the outbreak of the Civil War the principal wealth of North Carolina, according to historian Hugh Lefler, lay in some 350,000 slaves, whose value totaled more than a quarter of a billion dollars. The slave property owned by a small minority of wealthy white plantation owners exceeded the total value of land in the State, but yielded far less in taxes. For example, according to Lefler, "a thousand-dollar slave meant a tax of eighty cents to his owner, while a thousand-dollar cash income in salaries and wages was taxed six dollars, and a thousand dollars worth of land was taxed two dollars."[30] This inequity in taxation had begun to inspire hostile feelings among the State's approximately 200,000 laborers, farmers, and skilled tradesmen toward the 32,000 slave owners, long before the rebel shots at Fort Sumter.

The Civil War wiped out the evil institution of slavery and without labor to work the land, the land itself became worth less, causing even more stress for the State's treasury.

Treasurer Kemp Battle, the academic type among us, lamented in his report to the General Assembly in 1866 about the gross inequities of the property tax as it was levied and collected in his time. He wrote, "After independence was achieved, for many decades of years, land and polls, stud horses, jackasses and pedlars [*sic*] and occasionally billiard tables, had the exclusive honor of supporting the government of the State and its counties. In 1814, merchants were added, and at various times, anterior to 1848, were introduced Negro trades, jewelers, turnpike roads, brokers, and tavern keepers. In 1848, when the State embarked on extensive expenditures for Internal Improvements, the financial net was extended to bring in monied capital, investments in trading, salaries, and gold and silver plate. The income tax was added in 1849 but the law was nullified by the construction, not warranted, perhaps that income from property taxed in any other manner was exempt. This construction enabled all, except professional men to avoid the law."[31]

The erudite Treasurer Battle continued his argument for tax equity, "It is impossible to believe, yet such was the fact that from the close of the Revolution until 1814, land was taxed according to quantity, so that an

[30]Lefler and Newsome, *The History of a Southern State,* 367.
[31]Department of State Treasurer, *Treasurer's Report* 1886,3.

acre of barren huckleberry land on Mt. Pisgah paid the same tax as an acre in the fertile bottoms of the Roanoke." From 1814 to 1834, the assessment on land was according to its value, which was ascertained by the owner. This led to such extensive frauds that in 1834, on the recommendation of Governor Swain, whose message to the General Assembly that year pointed out in strong terms the inequalities and crudities of the revenue laws then existing, the present plan of valuation, by freeholders selected for the purpose was adopted.

Battle concluded there existed at the time he served as Treasurer, "enormous frauds in the listing of taxables." For example, he noted that between 1861 and 1866, some 3.5 million acres of land in 86 counties, worth a total of $15 million, had vanished from the tax rolls. There was also a decrease of more than 5,000 in the number of adult males subject to the poll tax between 1861 and 1866. Even the value of jackasses decreased by about one-third.

Battle suggested that the State ought to make a concerted effort to become more efficient in the collection of taxes and to establish a uniform method for assigning value and rates of taxes. In time, the State took his advice, but not for several years after the Reconstruction era.

Income Tax Becomes Real in 1921

For the first time, North Carolina enacted in 1921 a general net income tax which applied to all individuals and all incomes, except for a few exclusions, including capital gains. Also, there were a few special deductions, in addition to the personal exemptions.

The initial tax rates were modest: one percent for the first $2,500; one and one-half percent for the next $2,500; two percent for the next $2,500; two and one-half percent for the next $2,500 and three percent for income over $10,000. Personal exemptions allowable were: $1,000 for a single individual, $2,000 for a married person, widow or widower with a minor child or children, and children who were the head of a household; $1,000 for fiduciaries and $200 for each dependent other than spouse.

The major impact of this new income tax would not be felt for several decades since the per capita income in North Carolina in the 1920s was about $300 per year.

Revenue Act of 1933

Another important revision of the State's tax policy occurred in 1933. Acting in a moment of great crisis to relieve the epic of economic chaos which had spread across North Carolina, as it had across the nation, the General Assembly enacted the sales tax and set the initial rate at three percent. Revenue from the sales tax was used to fund the State's assumption of the cost of operating public schools, building roads and maintaining a statewide, centralized prison system. Between 1928 and 1932, revenue from the income tax declined by one-fifth, yet within two years of enacting the sales tax, North Carolina's general fund revenue surged by $9 million, an increase of almost one-third.

A New Trend Begins in the 1960s

I believe future historians, when they look back on the last half of this century, will see the emergence of a third phase in the evolution of North Carolina's tax policy. Beginning in the mid-1960s, there has been a tax explosion in this State and in this nation. President Lyndon Johnson moved quickly to launch the "Great Society" which set off an era of escalating entitlements–dramatic increases in Social Security, expanded welfare benefits and the creation of Medicare–free medical care for the aged, and Medicaid–free medical care for the poor. President Johnson persuaded Congress to raise taxes to pay for his social programs, which he called the "War on Poverty," and to fund the War in Vietnam at the same time. We lost both wars.

The "War on Poverty" was the beginning of a great escalation of government spending and a new direction for taxation policy in this country at both the national and state levels. Before the "War on Poverty" and other "Great Society" programs began in the mid-1960s, public funds were collected primarily to pay for necessary and essential government expenditures–defense, infrastructure and public safety. With the "Great Society" programs began a massive redistribution effort which sought to transfer wealth. Initially, the transfer was limited primarily from the very wealthy to the very poor. That has changed dramatically in the past three decades so that the transfer of resources today takes from everyone who works, including the working poor, and gives to everyone entitled to receive. In too many cases, the recipients are wealthy and do not need–much less deserve–government generosity. For example, the giant agribusiness conglomerates do not really deserve many of the overly generous federal farm subsidies which have been written in stone in the government farm price support programs, yet they are there and almost impossible to reduce or eliminate. Neither does the wealthy Medicare recipient deserve to have the government pay for his medical bills with funds that are taken from struggling young workers, many of whom cannot afford minimum medical care for their families.

Until 1960, the federal government had little involvement in what had been considered until that time to be the purview of the states, such as medical, health and education programs. Except for Social Security, enacted during the administration of President Franklin D. Roosevelt, these social programs were considered to be the responsibility of the states.

Development of our interstate highway system was the nation's first major federal initiative to become involved in an area which had been the domain of the states. The interstate highway system was begun in the mid-1950s under the leadership of President Dwight D. Eisenhower, who had seen the great autobahns of Europe and realized what such a system of interstate transportation could do to move America ahead. Then, in 1957, the Soviet Union launched "Sputnik," the first satellite to orbit the earth, and we were embarrassed that our own education system had been "shamed." The little Soviet satellite from our arch enemy inspired a massive national effort to improve public education in America, with help from the federal government. The federal role in education today involves a relatively small amount of money and lots of cumbersome regulations.

It was primarily the "Great Society" programs of Lyndon Johnson which led to the great increases in social spending. At first, these programs began as genuine and sincere efforts to provide relief to the neediest of our citizens. Since that modest start, however, these entitlement programs have been expanded and extended to millions more than were originally intended to benefit.

Real growth during the 1960s and 1980s provided a great deal more government revenue at both the federal and state levels to pay for these popular programs. During the 1970s, economic growth slowed (once during a recession and then again due to the Arab oil embargo) but inflation kicked in and provided more dollars, which were eagerly received by tax collectors. Entitlement programs, particularly social security, were expanded at rates far faster than the rate of real economic growth and, in some cases, faster than inflation. The result was a huge escalation in social spending.

President Ronald Reagan promised to balance the budget during his 1980 campaign, but when he left office eight years later, still a popular man, the federal budget was more out of balance than ever. In fact, the national debt increased during the combined terms of Presidents Reagan and George Bush by more than $1.5 trillion. These two conservative Presidents have the dubious honor of seeing the national debt grow by a sum larger than all their predecessors combined during the entire 200-year history of the Republic.

The huge Reagan-Bush deficits resulted from a mistaken belief, advocated by the executive branch, and reluctantly agreed to by the legislative branch, that lower taxes would generate sufficient increases in government revenue to pay for both increased social spending and a massive buildup of the defense infrastructure at the same time. The so-called "trickle-down" theory promoted by Reagan economists argued that tax breaks for the wealthy and coupled with huge defense expenditures by the government would combine to create a healthy economy that would add to the government coffers without a tax increase. It did not work. This theory did not work so well, in fact, that when President Bush agreed to a tax increase midway during his term, reneging on a bold campaign pledge made in 1988–"Read My Lips: No New Taxes," voters rewarded him with early retirement in 1992.

The four years of President Bush's term in office and the first year or so of President Clinton's term can be characterized as a period of low or modest growth and low inflation. The result is that there is little new revenue with which to expand government programs, except through real tax increases. Taxpayers have begun to resist tax increases. Ask Mr. Bush.

Beneficiaries of the various entitlement programs, Medicare, Medicaid, and government pensioners, grew accustomed to the generous increases of the 1980s, which were fueled by a combination of growth in the economy and inflation, and now feel abandoned because their doles were not increasing very much each year. Federal and state employees who were accustomed to getting substantial cost-of-living wage increases during the 1970s and 1980s were disappointed in subsequent years with more modest increases, and some years with no increases at all.

The solution to this dilemma must be better management of public funds. In the absence of real economic growth and in the face of growing demands for more government action to improve schools, combat crime, and provide a better quality of health care for all Americans, federal, state and local officials, have to eliminate the waste in their programs and, from these savings, develop new or expanded services with which to respond to public needs. In the absence of such a transformation of government, we face the threat of a real crisis in this nation. Already, there has been a great erosion of public confidence in the ability of government at all levels to do the job it is supposed to do.

The public perception of government is that of a bloated bureaucracy of too many, lethargic and overpaid workers, mainly concerned with their paychecks and pensions and little concerned with doing their jobs. That is an unfair and unwarranted assessment, because most public servants I have known over my four decades in public service have been hard-working, dedicated, and conscientious people. My colleagues and associates in the Treasurer's Office these past years include some of the brightest and most competent people found in either the public or private sector. There are equally dedicated workers, I'm confident, in most other government agencies.

However, there have been a few incidents of inept political appointments, misuse of power and greed on the part of a few people which have given a bad impression for the vast majority of hard-working public employees. Media accounts of these aberrations, unfortunately, have gotten wide attention and have tarnished the image of public employees in general.

In spite of the good intentions of "Great Society" programs and after more than a trillion dollars in relief programs, poverty and ignorance abound today in greater quantity than they did three decades ago. This failure has led to a direct and dire consequence for North Carolina taxpayers. It has been necessary to raise taxes substantially to pay for the State's share of federally mandated programs. Taxes will continue to go up because of these programs until drastic changes are made in our tax and expenditure policies. The reason these imprudent policies are in place today and have flourished is that the promoters and beneficiaries of these public expenditures have been successful in selling often exaggerated and much imagined benefits while minimizing the costs. Taxpayers have been poorly represented during the debates and discussions in the Congress and state legislature which led to such public largess. Only now, in the twilight of the 20th century when our national treasury is broke and taxes at state and local levels are becoming a crushing burden on middle-class families have we started to examine the issue thoroughly.

Table 4-1. North Carolina General Fund Tax Revenue by Category and State's Population for Selected Years, 1912-1994
(millions)

	Income Tax	Sales Tax	Other	Total	Population
1912	.044	–	2.06	2.1	2.2
1920	.498	–	6.5	7.0	2.6
1930	7.50	–	7.8	15.3	3.2
1940	11.30	11.6	16.2	39.1	3.6
1950	60.0	47.0	33.0	140.0	4.1
1960	101.0	82.0	73.0	256.0	4.6
1970	380.0	265.0	197.0	842.0	5.1
1980	1,471.0	692.0	476.0	2,639.0	5.9
1990	3,957.6	1,767.7	848.2	6,573.5	6.6
1994	4,254.5	2,578.8	1,703.2	8,536.5	7.0

Source: North Carolina Department of Revenue, *State Taxation Reports, Biennium Budget Reports.*

Figure 4-1. North Carolina General Fund by Source of Funds, Fiscal Year 1993-94

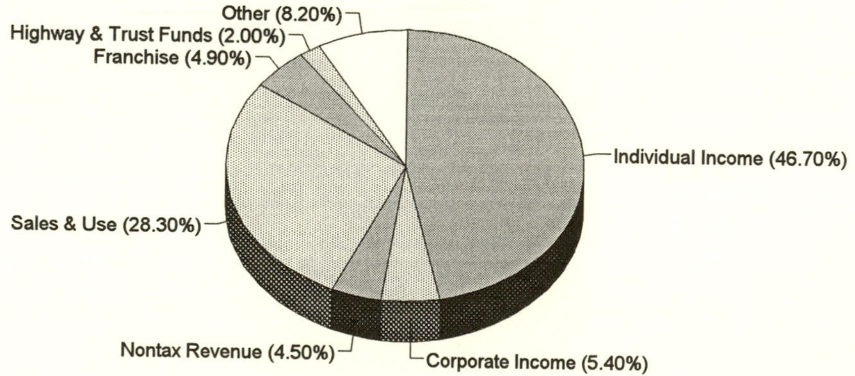

Table 4-2. History of the North Carolina Income Tax

1849 - State's first income tax applied only to interest, dividends and some profits plus professional fees and salaries over $500.

1921 - First income tax law applying to all individuals and almost all income, except for capital gains.

First $2,500 - 1 percent
Next $2,500 - 1.5 percent
Next $2,500 - 2 percent
Next $2,500 - 2.5 percent
Over $10,000 - 3 percent

1925 - Rates were increased:
First $2,500 - 1.25 percent
Next $2,500 - 2 percent
Next $2,500 - 2.75 percent
Next $2,500 - 3.50 percent
Next $5,000 - 4.5 percent
Over $15,000 - 5%

1931 - Rates were increased:
First $2,000 - 2 percent
Next $2,000 - 3 percent
Next $2,000 - 4 percent
Next $2,000 - 5 percent
Next $2,000 - 5.5 percent
Over $10,000 - 6 percent

1933 - Rates were increased:
First $2,000 - 3 percent
Next $2,000 - 4 percent
Next $2,000 - 5 percent
Over $6,000 - 6 percent

1937 - Rates were increased:
First $2,000 - 3 percent
Next $2,000 - 4 percent
Next $2,000 - 5 percent
Next $4,000 - 6 percent
Over $10,000 - 7 percent

1989 - North Carolina's individual income tax was restructured to use federal taxable income as the starting point for computation of State taxable income.

Married, filing jointly,
First $21,250 - 6 percent
Over $21,250 - 7 percent

Married filing separately
First $10,625 - 6 percent
Over $10, 625 - 7 percent

Head of household
First $17,000 - 6 percent
Over $17,000 - 7 percent

Single
First $12,750 - 6 percent
Over $12,750 - 7 percent

1991 - Rates were raised:
Married filing jointly
First $21,250 - 6 percent
Next $78,750 - 7 percent
Over $100,000 - 7.75 percent

Married filing separately
First $10,625 - 6 percent
Next $39,375 - 7 percent
Over $50,000 - 7.75 percent
Single
First $12,750 - 6 percent
Next $47,250 - 7 percent
Over $60,000 - 7.75 percent

The State Revenue 1994

Not counting highway user taxes and license fees, North Carolina taxes generated $9.4 billion in General Fund revenue in fiscal 1993. The personal income tax and sales tax together account for three-quarters of the total State tax collections. In fiscal 1993, personal income taxes were responsible for half of the State's total revenue and sales taxes brought in an additional 30 percent. In 1912, the $44,114 income taxes collected accounted for only two percent of the total General Fund collections of $2.1 million. Business taxes, which generated 35 percent of the total State revenue in 1935, now account for only a small portion of the State's General Fund revenue. The corporate income tax, which generated 25 percent of the State's total General Fund revenue in 1935 has declined now to only five percent of the General Fund.

Summary

North Carolina's concept of taxation has been an evolutionary process dating back from the early Colonial Days. The State's leaders traditionally have been reluctant to use taxes except for the very essential and necessary public services. That was the clear public policy for nearly 200 years. However, beginning in the late 1960s the taxes paid by North Carolina citizens have been increasing faster than any other item in the family budget.

Between 1960 and 1992, North Carolina's population increased 50 percent. The cost of living index increased 4.7 times. Yet the State budget increased by a factor of 24.

The story is in the numbers.

Chapter 5

Other Sources of Revenue: Debt, Licenses, Fees and Nontax Revenues

Neither a borrower nor a lender be, For loan oft loses both itself and friend, And borrowing dulls the edge of husbandry.

Polonius's Speech to His Son
in Shakespeare's *Hamlet*

In regard to the matter of public debt, North Carolina leaders have followed the advice of the bard, with two notable exceptions. That policy has contributed significantly to our fiscal integrity, now the envy of the nation. One exception was during the Great Depression when a nationwide decline in revenue left both the State and most local governments without the resources to pay their bills. The other exception was during the Reconstruction Era, just after the Civil War, when railroad bonds were issued fraudulently to benefit a few officeholders and their patrons. These bonds were later repudiated.

Debt has always been a word reluctantly used in North Carolina. Perhaps it is because of the horror stories handed down from ancestors who suffered in debtors' prison in Europe, which they then fled in disgrace and with an abject hatred for the continent, its customs and the particular vice that had gotten them in trouble. Has that abhorrence for the concept of debt been handed down from generation to generation? Perhaps it has. Or perhaps, we are inherently a thrifty people.

Much has been said and written about the public debt in recent years. Our national leaders during the 1980s followed a policy of public finance which resulted in the accumulation of more debt in one decade than the country had acquired during the entire previous history of the republic. This happened during the term of a President who campaigned promising to balance the budget and begin paying off previous debt. That debt now hangs ominously above our nation, a gigantic burden on the shoulders of future generations.

North Carolina has one of the best records of any state in the country in controlling and managing its public debt. Our low debt is a major factor in our Triple-A credit rating.

As of June 30, 1993, the State's bonded indebtedness, including funds owed by county and city governments and special tax districts was $5.1 billion. Of that amount the State owed $581 million. In addition, there was $11.5 billion outstanding in revenue bonds. The State debt was less than one twentieth of the gross state product as compared with the national debt which just about equals the gross national product. In per capita State debt, which is $84 in North Carolina, we rank in the bottom five of all states. The per capita national debt is $17,000.

North Carolina leaders have used debt sparingly in critical situations to build needed, long-term improvements. In 1840, in a bold and then highly controversial move, the Governor and General Assembly borrowed the equivalent of two full years' revenue to build the new State Capitol. In its day, it was one of the most glorious buildings in all America.

In 1921, North Carolina voters approved a $50 million highway bond issue, a massive undertaking for that time. These funds, along with a modest gasoline tax, were used to build a network of hard-surfaced roads connecting the 100 county seats in this State. This was the State's first venture into road building, which previously had been the responsibility of the counties.

In 1949 Governor W. Kerr Scott fulfilled his promise to farmers to get them out of the mud with a network of farm-to-market roads. This time, voters were asked, and they approved a $200 million highway bond issue which was used to pave some 15,000 miles of secondary roads and stabilize an additional 15,000 miles of farm-to-market roads.

More recently, voters have been asked to approve, and they have given their support for bond financing to build new prisons and to improve our public universities and community colleges. Each of these types of expenditures is considered a bonafide investment in the future.

There are two good reasons for using debt. First, the process of borrowing money enables an individual, business or the public to make large purchases that would not be affordable otherwise. Long-lasting projects like highways, school buildings and other capital outlays are usually financed through debt. The use of debt for these kinds of purchases is both prudent and practical because of their long-term use, which justifies spreading out the payment over a long period of time.

And second, debt is a good idea for the borrower when there is reason to believe that it will paid off in cheaper dollars. The primary consequence of borrowing is to delay payment until a future time. When the buyer of public debt believes that he or she will gain from such an investment after calculating the interest payments they will receive plus special tax incentives offered for the purchase of government bonds, then both the borrower and the lender benefit.

Borrowing money to pay for current operations such as salaries for State employees or to pay for utility bills or office supplies is not a good practice and is prohibited by the Constitution. Current operations and services are defined as those which are used up during the current budget period, usually within one year. Take for example, the family without sufficient funds to pay for food and shelter for this month. If they borrow to get money for that purpose, what are they going to do next month? If they borrow again and again to pay current bills, eventually their credit will be exhausted, they will have no money and yet will have incurred a huge debt.

It has been our policy in North Carolina since the Great Depression to borrow as little money as we possibly could to avoid the problem of deferring our financial obligations to the future. Rather, we have chosen to fund projects, including many capital projects on a pay-as-you-go policy.

North Carolina's founding fathers were so concerned about the potential abuse of public debt that they wrote a special section into the Constitution limiting its use–Section 3 of Article V of the North Carolina Constitution. Specifically, this section prohibits the General Assembly from contracting debts secured by the faith and credit of taxpayers unless approved by a majority of voters. The constitution provides for incurring debt in only six ways, without a vote of the people. These exceptions include: (1) to fund or refund a valid existing debt; (2) to supply an unforeseen deficiency in revenue; (3) to borrow in anticipation of the collection of taxes due and payable within the current fiscal year to an amount not exceeding 50 percent of such taxes; (4) to suppress riots or insurrections, or to repel invasions; (5) to meet emergencies immediately threatening the public health or safety, as conclusively determined in writing by the Governor; and, (6) for any other lawful purpose, to the extent of two-thirds of the amount by which the State's outstanding indebtedness shall have been reduced during the next preceding biennium.

Bond Financing

The State occurs debt through the sale of bonds. A bond is a written understanding that, in exchange for a certain rate of interest and a specific repayment date, the buyer of the bond will provide a specific amount of cash to the borrower.

Table 5-1. North Carolina Bonds Issued 1900-1994

General Fund	
Higher Education	$263,250,000
Community Colleges	181,500,000
Public Schools	575,475,945
Hospitals	44,556,132
Prisons	314,815,836
Clean Water	381,555,000
Capital Projects	76,985,984
Refunding	354,545,000
Miscellaneous	84,344,531
Total	$2,277,528,433
Highway Fund	$1,196,995,000

The most frequent kind of bond used by State and local governments in North Carolina is general obligation bonds which are guaranteed by the "full faith and credit" of the governmental unit issuing the bond. In using this type of bond, the governmental unit pledges to repay the bond with interest, either by managing its fiscal affairs without a tax increase, but if necessary by raising taxes.

Another popular type of bond financing in recent years has been the revenue bond which is paid back with revenue from a specific project such as a parking deck, airport, or toll highway.

Deficit Financing

Deficit financing of the operating budget is strictly prohibited in North Carolina. Our Constitution requires a balanced operating budget and that is one of our greatest gifts to future generations.

Nontax Revenue

One area of the North Carolina State budget growing steadily and promising to exert an even greater influence upon public finance in this State is identified simply as "nontax revenue."

Table 5-2. History of North Carolina Highway Bonds, 1900-1994

Year	Amount	Purpose
1921	$50,000,000	Building a road network to connect county seats.
1923	$15,000,000	
1925	$20,000,000	
1925	$550,000	Chowan River Bridge
1927	$30,000,000	
1927	$1,250,000	Cape Fear River Bridge
1931		State assumed responsibility for all roads
1949	$200,000,000	
1965	$300,000,000	
1977	$300,000,000	
1983	$250,000,000	Highway Refunding Bonds
1993	$30,195,000	Highway Refunding Bonds

The cumulative total of North Carolina Highway bonds issued is $1,196,995,000.

In the 1993-94 budget nontax revenue totaled $353 million. That does not seem like a lot of money in a total budget of $16.7 billion. Actually, the sum is quite significant because of the future implications of the important role which nontax revenue will play. As taxpayers become more sensitive to increased income and sales taxes which go into the General Fund and are paying for a myriad of public services, State leaders will have to turn to more specific sources of revenue to fund future programs. The trend is to look for user fees that have a relationship between the users of a government-provided service and the service rendered.

Already, a number of State agencies are funded almost entirely by fees and assessments. The annual State Fair, sponsored each year by the Department of Agriculture, is a good example. The State Banking Commission, which regulates State-chartered banks, operates entirely from the assessments it levies against the banks it regulates.

The State Alcohol Beverage Control Board actually makes a substantial profit from the distribution and sale of spirituous liquor.

No doubt the success of these operations will give rise to implementation of other fees and assessments by agencies which serve a particular constituency. It is only fair that those who benefit from a service not enjoyed by all taxpayers should pay for that service.

Investment Income

Of the $353 million projected amount in nontax revenue in the 1993-94 budget, some $85 million is investment income generated by the Treasurer's Office. Investment income is a source of great pride for the Treasurer's Office because of the sense of achievement it gives the professional managers who use their expertise and ingenuity on behalf of the citizens of North Carolina.

This investment income is generated by investing temporarily idle State funds in short-term investments. Rather than allow revenue to sit idle in a bank account, these funds are invested daily. The result is a substantial amount of money, sufficient to fund several entire State government departments. In addition, the investment of other trust funds yields even greater dividends for State taxpayers; however, these proceeds are not shown in the annual budget because they are added to those trusts funds. More about that later.

Judicial Fees

Judicial fees account for $84.5 million in nontax revenue in the 1993-94 budget. These fees come from court costs assessed and constitute a valuable source of revenue for the over-burdened court system. Court fees will probably become an even greater source of revenue in the future as legislators look for more innovative ways to fund the expansion of our judicial system.

For example, the suggestion has been made that guilty persons who can afford to do so ought to be required to pay for their upkeep while they are guests of the State in prison. Such a policy would not only generate additional funds, it would serve as a further deterrent against crime.

Disproportionate State Share Receipts

There is in the budget a strange line item called "disproportionate State share receipts." This mysterious source accounted for some $93 million of revenue in the State budget in 1993, but disappeared entirely the following year. It was a reimbursement to the State for its share of overpaid Medicaid expenses in a previous year. At the time the General

Assembly discussed this item during its 1993 session, there was concern raised by the media that perhaps the State was using these funds inappropriately by spending them for purposes other than Medicaid. However, the General Assembly concluded this was a perfectly legal thing to do.

Miscellaneous

The 1993-94 budget contains a $90.4 million item for miscellaneous nontax revenue, an increase of $12.2 million from the previous year's budget. Included in this array of user fees and assessments are a wide variety of nontax revenue sources, which reflect a growing effort by the State to charge special beneficiaries of State services for the value of service rendered.

Major contributors to this account are the departments of Insurance, State Banking Commission, and Alcohol Beverage Control (ABC) Board, among others.

Perhaps the most efficient department, in terms of its negligible cost to taxpayers, is the State Banking Commission. This agency regulates State-chartered banks to see they remain solvent and are being operated in the public interest. One hundred percent of the cost of operating the State Banking Commission comes from fees assessed State-chartered banks. Its $3.8 million budget comes entirely from such assessments.

Perhaps the most aggressive use of nontax revenue is demonstrated by the ABC Board. It buys and sells 3.3 million cases of liquor at an enormous profit for both State and local government coffers. In fact, the nontax revenue generated by the ABC Board is sufficient to pay for the entire $6 million cost of running the State headquarters and warehouse operations. In a typical year the Board will issue approximately 45,000 ABC permits, cancel another 8,000, hold 750 hearings on allegations of ABC law violations, and conduct some 7,000 inspections to make sure the State's liquor laws are being obeyed. None of this important work costs taxpayers a dime. In fact, profit from the State-controlled distribution and sale of liquor yields millions of dollars in profits annually for local governments throughout the State. The ABC Board, as a State-sponsored monopoly, is one of the State's most profitable government operations. If only other departments could emulate the ABC Board. The potential for generating additional revenue for the courts, if lawyers were assessed a fee each time they used the court, is tremendous. And why not?

Already, a variety of government programs are funded with specific fees and assessments. A disposal fee is now charged for discarding scrap automobile tires and appliances. When convicted drunk drivers seek to get their driver's licenses restored, they must pay a fee which becomes a part of the State's nontax revenue fund, as do the fees which parolees pay for their court-ordered supervision.

Other Nontax Sources

A good argument can be made for identifying other revenues which the State already collects, bringing those accounts on-line in this category of the budget document. For example, the University system collects nearly $700 million in tuition fees each year. While that amount is reflected in the overall University budget, it does not appear anywhere except in brief mention as estimated receipts.

Should not tuition fees received by our University system be included in our total assessment of State nontax revenue? I think they should.

Again, the University Hospitals in Chapel Hill projected a total budget of $346 million for fiscal year 1993-94. Of that total, some $305 million was accounted for in receipts, leaving taxpayers with the burden of only having to pay $41 million of operating costs for teaching and patient care.

The University-operated hospital at Chapel Hill is nationally acclaimed as one of the great medical teaching institutions in America and truly should be counted among our State treasures. In fiscal year 1994-95, it anticipated some 23,000 admissions, more than 37,000 clinic visits and 41,400 emergency room visits. It employs 4,417 persons.

Yet the hospital's ultimate impact upon the State budget is the $41 million appropriation required. A more fair assessment would include the $305 million nontax revenue that is generated through patient fees, insurance reimbursements, and grants.

The same is true for revenue from hunting and fishing licenses, State Parks administration fees, and numerous other revenues generated by State programs. Outdoorsmen pay some $13 million a year for the privilege of taking fish from the fresh inland waters and hunting deer and bear. This is not tax revenue but a fee paid for services rendered in the form of State administration and protection of the fragile game and wildlife balance. A good argument can be made that people who enjoy fishing in sounds, tributaries and offshore waters of North Carolina ought to pay a similar fee for that privilege; however, none has ever been charged. It probably will be.

The Department of Agriculture is an excellent example of how nontax revenue can be generated to support needed public services. Nearly 40 percent of the department's budget in 1994 was generated by receipts, otherwise referred to as nontax revenue.

The State Fair, for example is self-sustaining. It costs approximately $6 million annually to stage. It generates $6 million in revenue from admissions and the rentals of booth space to exhibitors and vendors. The farmers' markets, operated by the Department of Agriculture are designed on a break-even basis, with users benefitting from the service being asked to pay for the necessary operation expenses.

The Department of Labor, which is charged with the important task of protecting workers, generates nearly one-third of its total cost of operation from inspection and other user fees.

The not-for-profit MicroElectronics Center of North Carolina (MCNC) raises more than half ($18.7 million) of its $34.7 million annual budget from customer charges.

Trust Fund Revenue

During the fiscal year ending June 30, 1993, total earnings from the investments of all retirement funds managed by the Treasurer's Office exceeded $2.0 billion. Although these funds are properly accounted for in the various trust funds, should the value of investment earnings not be reflected in the total nontax revenue? The total value of these nontax revenue items–university tuition, university hospital receipts, and trust funds investments–accounts for nearly $3 billion of nontax revenue that is not presently reflected in the State budget.

Recommendations

Nontax revenue will play an increasingly important role in future State budget operations. As taxpayers become more sophisticated about the value of public spending on their behalf, they will scrutinize programs more closely and cause some programs to be trimmed or deleted altogether. State managers will have to get accustomed to a higher degree of accountability than they've known in the past because taxpayers are demanding more and more accountability in the appropriation of public funds. Nontax funds, also, are public funds.

Agencies which pay their own way (through user fees, assessments and other self-generated "nontax" revenues) are the tide of the future.

Chapter 6

The State's Money: Where Does It Go?

The spending choices of a government reflect its true character. Watch where the money goes and that will tell you clearer than all the platitudes praised and passed where the heart and soul of a society really exist.

The authorized budget for the State of North Carolina in fiscal year 1994 (July 1, 1993 - June 30, 1994) was $16.7 billion. That is a lot of money, especially for a modestly progressive southern State, as we have preferred to see ourselves for a generation or so. This averages out to an annual expenditure of nearly $2,500 for each man, woman and child who reside in our State. For working taxpayers, the burden is much higher.

The spending choices which a government makes are a true reflection of its character, its priorities, and its values. Far more important than the platitudes it enacts, far more important than the resolutions it passes, and more important than either the recommendations of its study commissions or the findings of white papers, is where government actually spends its money. The age-old advice, "watch the money and where the money goes, there is the truth," is as valid for government as it is for every other human endeavor.

Through its spending choices, government exercises its most powerful tool for setting public policy. Again watch where the money goes and you will see where the heart and soul of a government's priorities exist.

In North Carolina, the spending of public funds is governed by two sections of Article V of the State Constitution which deal with finance. Section 2, paragraph 1 stipulates that "The power of taxation shall be exercised in a just and equitable manner, for public purposes only..." Section 7, paragraph 1, further stipulates, "No money shall be drawn from the State Treasury but in consequence of appropriations made by law, and an accurate account of the receipts and expenditures of State funds shall be published annually."

North Carolina's Constitution dictates that its public funds can only be used for public purposes, specifically authorized by the General Assembly, and that a strict accounting must be made for all expenditures.

In the early, formative years of the development of our agrarian State, only the very essential matters of public concern—chiefly public safety and the operation of a bare-bones government—were deemed to meet the definition of the Constitution's "public purpose" requirement and thereby justify the expenditure of public funds.

The major item in the North Carolina budget for many years was the cost of biennial sessions of the General Assembly. In 1840, when the present State Capitol was built in Raleigh, it housed the entire executive and legislative branches of North Carolina government. Construction of the Capitol stirred strong protests even though it was generally thought to be the most beautiful example of Greek architecture in the nation; its $540,000 cost then represented the State's total revenues for nearly two years.

Today, the $25 million annual appropriation of the General Assembly to fund itself is but a tiny portion of the total State budget. Education, public assistance, highways, law and order, health, welfare, economic development, medical bills of its poor citizens, and preserving the natural resources of this great State have all become major public purposes as evidenced by the use of the State's public monies.

There are many anomalies in the State's spending. For example, the State of North Carolina purchases $200 million worth of hard whiskey each year which is sold through county operated ABC stores to its citizens in a carefully controlled manner, and at a fat profit for local governments. This makes the State, in the opinion of some, the pusher of a highly abused drug.

The State owns and operates (ostensibly for the public purpose) a railroad, a motor fleet of 5,500 cars, and a small air force of three executive aircraft used primarily for the convenience and efficiency of the Governor and other top State officials.

Through its public schools, North Carolina operates the State's largest public transit system (school busses) and the largest cafeteria food service, which serves nearly a million lunches daily. Through its Department of Human Resources, the State of North Carolina is the State's largest provider of health care, dispensing billions of dollars annually to the State's hospitals, doctors, rest homes, nursing homes, and other providers of medical care for the State's poor and aged.

The State of North Carolina is the largest employer, within its boundaries, providing jobs for 217,000 people in 1993, an increase of 41 percent in just seven years. State jobs are among the best jobs in North

Table 6-1. North Carolina Budget, Fiscal Year 1993-94

General Assembly		$ .025 billion
Education		
Public Schools	4.2 billion	
University System	1.8 billion	
Community Colleges	.5 billion	
Total Education		6.500 billion
Human Resources		5.300 billion
Transportation		1.700 billion
Justice		
Courts	250 million	
Law enforcement	500 million	
Prisons	550 million	
Total Justice		1.300 billion
Environment/Health		.500 billion
General Government and others		.375 billion
Debt Service		.130 billion
Misc Reserves & Transfers		.550 billion
Capital Improvements		.350 billion
	TOTAL	$16.700 billion

Figure 6-1. General Fund Operating Budget, Fiscal Year 1993-94

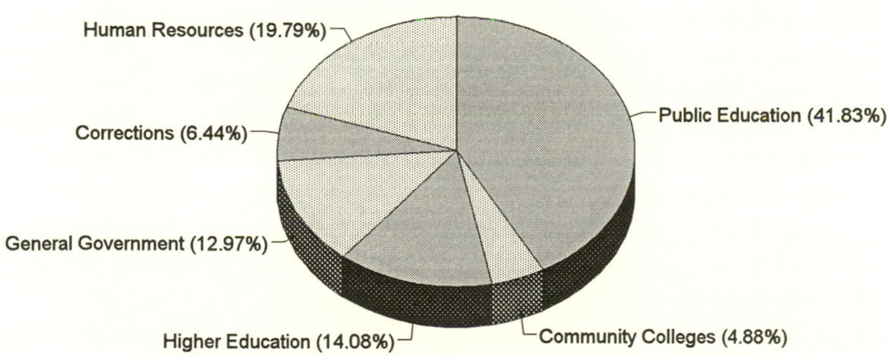

Carolina, providing good pay, excellent benefits such as health insurance, regular pay increases, a sound pension program and, best of all, excellent job security.

Education

In fiscal year 1994, we spent more of our State budget, $6.5 billion, for education than any other purpose. No one, in this day when education is valued as a means to a better quality of life for our sons and daughters, would question whether public support of education is a worthy public purpose. It is that indeed. And, it is entirely appropriate that we have decided our children are our top priority by our decision to spend more on their future potential than any other item in the North Carolina budget. But it is a legitimate question to ask: "Are we getting good value for the education dollars we spend?"

Great University System

North Carolina's public university system is generally regarded as one of the very best in the nation. The University of North Carolina became the first State university in the young nation when it opened for business in 1795, and has grown to a nationally renowned institution, now serving 152,000 students–130,000 full-time–on 16 campuses spread across the entire State. Our University system has been a source of great native pride from the day of its humble origin, when William R. Davie and his Presbyterian friends conceived the idea of a great institution of higher learning. They did not think then of the University as a place of universal opportunity, as it is today. North Carolina's university system began under the heavy influence of Presbyterian clergy who promoted the institution as a place where its ministers could be trained to understand and preach the scriptures of the Bible. Although the newly adopted Constitution of the United States clearly dictated the policy of separation of church and state, that policy was construed in the early days of the Republic as meaning freedom from having to worship in the Church of England, as formerly dictated under British rule.

The University prospered for a century and a half as a place where the State's affluent and intellectual white citizens sent their male offspring. Not until the mid-1900s, when thousands of young Tar Heel veterans of World War II began returning home with GI educational assistance from a thankful and benevolent nation, did a college education became a realistic dream for everyone wanting to learn.

Today, our public university system in North Carolina consists of 16 campuses which employ 32,000 people, boasts two medical schools (one of them nationally acclaimed) and conducts world-class, high-tech research and training. It has attained outstanding achievements in the arts, not to mention consistent excellence on basketball courts and gridirons. These are valid reasons for great pride and confidence among all citizens of the State. The University's $1.8 billion budget in fiscal 1994, an average expenditure of $13,683 for each full-time student enrolled, is perceived to be one of the State's best public expenditures.

North Carolina Public Schools

Our public schools in North Carolina, however, are not held in such high esteem as our institutions of higher learning.

An evaluation by the North Carolina Department of Public Instruction in early 1994 revealed that 60 percent of all high school students in the State were performing at less than a satisfactory level of performance. North Carolina students have traditionally ranked low in national achievement tests. In 1989, when North Carolina SAT scores sank to 50th in the nation, a great outcry arose from public and business leaders, embarrassed by the suggestion that low SAT scores meant we had the worst secondary schools in the nation. Industrial recruiters were especially concerned that their efforts to recruit new business and industry might be set back by the bad news about our schools. The howls continued for a year, until our SAT scores rose to 48th and then public concern quieted, apparently in the consensus that it is okay to be almost last, just not last.

The implications of inadequate public schools, especially in view of the fact that we're spending more money on public education than any other part of the budget, are far reaching. Underachieving students will become underachieving adults. They will either remain unemployable if they graduate from high school, or become employed at below median wages. The specter of a huge portion of our population remaining either unemployed or under employed will have dire consequences for the quality of life for future generations. The consequences of an inferior education system upon the State's finances are profound and significant. As a result of their diminished earnings, many high school dropouts and underachievers will not become productive citizens. Instead of becoming taxpayers, they will become tax users. In many cases, they will not be able to find jobs at all and may become wards of the State, either on the burgeoning welfare rolls or in prison.

There have been four great initiatives on behalf of advancing public education in the history of North Carolina. Hillsboro attorney Archibald Murphey first suggested to his fellow legislators in 1817 that North Carolina ought to do better by its children and assume the burden of their education, which at that time was solely a private matter for each family. Since only the very wealthy families could afford even a minimal education for their offspring, most of our citizens grew up illiterate. Twenty years after Murphey first suggested his radical ideas, the legislature warmed up to the notion that public education was a worthy endeavor and began to implement a few of his recommendations, such as public support for a system of "common" schools. The office of the State Superintendent of Public Instruction was created largely to rally public support for education. Significant progress in a uniform system of public schools was made in the late 1840s and 1850s, only to be disrupted by the Civil War.

Governor Charles B. Aycock was elected in 1900 in a bold campaign to improve public schools. Access to education for the State's black and white children was the major goal of his four-year term. He succeeded immensely. When his term was finished, one new school had been built, on the average, for each day that he served. It was an incredible achievement. Admittedly primitive by today's standards, many of them consisted of a single room where all students gathered around a wood stove in the winter months and one teacher taught all students in the community. But it was a start.

Governor Terry Sanford renewed North Carolina's commitment to public schools in the early 1960s with his pledge to increase teacher pay and by the creation of the community college system, first suggested by Governor Luther Hodges. The community college system was begun as a series of technical institutes focused primarily upon teaching job skills to high school graduates not going to a liberal arts college or university.

Basic Education Program

The most significant recent education boost came from the enactment of the Basic Education Program (BEP) in 1985, which promised an infusion of more than $800 million annually into the public schools budget over an eight-year period. The purpose of the program was to guarantee every child in North Carolina access to a "basic education" regardless of where he or she lived. The BEP expanded the concept of the 3 "Rs" to include music, art and technology. By doing so, the standard course of study and the purposes for which the State would pay instructional costs were also expanded and enlarged. This new concept and new money was touted as the panacea for all of education's problems. A decade after the BEP was first enacted, its results have been hard to measure. Well before the BEP was fully funded and its provisions implemented, the General Assembly retreated from its earlier commitment, and probably rightfully so.

The primary strategy which the BEP offered to North Carolina's education was the addition of 40,000 new education employees, many of them non-teachers. While the BEP did put additional math and science teachers in poor, rural schools across the State, it also gave added emphasis to art teachers, counselors, administrators, and clerks. The BEP failed to achieve its goal of dramatically improving the quality of our public schools for several reasons.

First, it did not raise standards for either the students or for the new personnel. This was an excellent opportunity for the General Assembly to have tied the new funding to higher performance standards.

Second, its goals did not focus sharply on the two main problems which have plagued our schools for two decades–declining student achievement and increased dropouts.

Third, the BEP did not attempt to restructure the education system which operates essentially the same today as it has for a century. The BEP simply added more money and more employees to a system which urgently needs to be changed.

Between 1975 and 1995, the budget of our public schools grew from under $1 billion to more than $4 billion. Public school employment during the same period almost doubled while the number of students actually declined slightly from the 1.1 million enrollment of two decades ago. So, the solution to the problem of our underachieving schools is neither more money nor more school employees.

Most of the operational money we spend on education (84%) is spent for salaries of the 131,000 school employees. Our school payroll in 1994 was more than $4 billion and, sadly to say, we employed more administrators and support personnel than teachers. That is one of the things which needs to be changed if we are to improve our schools. Second, we have not made a diligent effort to recruit, train, certify and keep good teachers. The teachers' union has successfully persuaded the legislature to ignore most efforts to make meaningful changes in North Carolina schools, except for adding new employees and increasing salaries. Genuine efforts to improve the quality of our schools by improving the quality of teachers, setting higher standards for students, and systemic reforms in the structure of our schools have been stymied by those who are comfortable with the status quo, in spite of the fact that it leaves many of our young generation with an inferior education.

This is an area of the budget where battles will continue to be fought until legislators and taxpayers come to believe they are getting a better value from their education tax dollars.

Already, the consequence of our poor schools is being manifested, in the exploding burden upon North Carolina's treasury by the growing prison population and by the rising cost of our welfare program.

Public Assistance

The second largest, and fastest growing, item in the North Carolina 1994 budget was the $5.3 billion appropriation for the Department of Human Resources (DHR). By the year 2000, possibly sooner if this area of the budget continues to expand at its current pace, public assistance will account for North Carolina's largest category of public spending. Most of the funds spent by this department ($4.1 billion) are federal funds, and though they come from Washington, they are tax monies nevertheless coming out of the pockets and from the toil of our citizens. The money that is returned to North Carolina from Washington is less than the amount we send, after it has been reduced by the feeding and care of Washington bureaucrats and siphoned off to fund other programs. In 1994, for example, we sent to Washington $1.20 for each dollar that we received back in federal aid.

The North Carolina Department of Human Resources employs more than 16,700 people and is the State's largest centralized agency. (Although there are more teachers and other education employees, they are employed by local boards of education, though funded by the State.) DHR operates a myriad of complex and diverse public assistance programs: chief among them are Medicaid, which provides medical care for the poor, and Aid for Families with Dependent Children (AFDC), more commonly known as "welfare." The department's mission is described in the 1993-95 State budget document: "The Department of Human Resources provides services that benefit all North Carolina citizens as individuals, families and communities in their efforts to achieve and maintain health, social and economic well-being, and self-respect. This is done by communication to develop understanding, coordination of efforts, and cooperation with private and public entities to identify opportunities and focus resources. Strategies emphasize prevention and preparedness, strengthening families, welfare of children and older adults, consideration of individual differences and encouragement of independence and self reliance."

The Department achieves its goals, primarily by dispensing money. Through this giant bureaucracy flow billions of dollars each year to the poor, those unable to work, and in some cases, those unwilling to work.

Medicaid

The growing burden of Medicaid expenditures presents an even greater concern. Medicaid expenditures in North Carolina increased by a half-billion dollars annually during the first half of the 1990s and accounted for $3.2 billion in the final 1994 State budget. Between 1988 and 1993, the average annual cost per Medicaid recipient in North Carolina increased only 20 percent, from $3,079 to $3,711; however, other factors have emerged to propel a program growing at a pace that threatens to bankrupt governments at both national and state/local levels.

Three reasons explain the dramatic increase–increased enrollment, higher medical costs, and a declining economy. First, the number of eligible Medicaid recipients doubled in North Carolina between 1988 and 1993, increasing from 304,000 to 657,000. Second, higher medical costs in general and the special needs of many Medicaid patients are a major reason for the program's dramatic growth. Although the number of elderly and disabled beneficiaries represent a small percent of the total Medicaid beneficiaries, the higher costs associated with their acute needs and long-term care is a major factor in the escalating costs of the program. And third, the recession of the early 1990s added significantly to the rolls of those entitled to have their medical bills paid by Medicaid.

Adding to Medicaid's difficulties are the astronomical costs of some medical procedures which were considered experimental just a few years ago, but are now almost routine. For example, heart, liver and lung transplants costing $100,000 and more are becoming routine procedures within the State Medicaid program.

In 1993, the State Medicaid program paid Presbyterian Hospital in Pittsburgh, Pennsylvania, $310,000 to install a liver in a 41-year-old patient. In 1990, Children's Hospital in Pittsburgh was paid $339,000 for a liver transplant received by a two-year-old infant who died.

Between 1989 and 1994, the UNC Hospital in Chapel Hill performed most of the expensive organ transplant operations funded by the State's

Medicaid program, accounting for 42 heart, liver, and lung transplants, at an average cost of $65,000 per procedure. Duke Medical Center ranked second with 29 operations, averaging $60,000 each. During that same period of time, the private, not-for-profit Carolinas Medical Center in Charlotte was third, with 11 transplants at an average cost of $64,000 each. The Children's Hospital in Pittsburgh performed nine transplants involving North Carolina Medicaid patients, at an average cost of $140,000 each.

There is no way to predict future costs of this program since it is open-ended, meaning that all those who meet the criteria to have their medical bills paid by Medicaid can present themselves for treatment, and it is provided.

Medicaid illustrates the best and the worst of the concept of federalism, an evolving partnership between federal, state and local governments seeking to find the best way to serve the needs of America's citizens. The 65 percent share of Medicaid costs which the federal government pays seems like a generous gesture, leaving the State to pay 20 percent and 15 percent by the counties. However, Medicaid is an open-ended entitlement program in which the federal government sets the rules for those who qualify and then forces the State and county governments to pay their share of the bill, regardless of how large the amount. This single federal mandate already has caused budgeting difficulties for the State and is resulting in serious problems for many poor, rural counties which are cutting back in other local spending programs, including education, just to raise their mandated share of Medicaid expenditures.

Making the problem even worse is the fact that the federal government can resort to heavy borrowing to fund its share of current expenses, thus deferring the ultimate burden of payment for future generations, while State and local governments must balance their budgets annually.

Welfare

Welfare expenditures doubled during the 1980s and now command a larger appropriation than did the entire State budget just three decades ago. The 1994 budget includes $1.1 billion for welfare payments to the State's citizens through a variety of programs, Aid For Families with Dependent Children, job training, refugee assistance, energy assistance, child adoption programs, foster care, etc. Though the average monthly welfare payment is small, $230 in 1994, the sheer number of recipients, which averaged 340,000, compounds to a huge total cost.

Rather than strengthening the family, there is a growing consensus that welfare policies–which prohibit households with an employed male from receiving certain welfare assistance–have caused the breakup of poor families. Cited as proof is the increase in the number of poor households headed by single mothers and the dramatic increase in the number of children born to unwed mothers since the birth of "Great Society" welfare programs in 1968. As recently as 1982, one in five of all births in North Carolina were to unmarried mothers. By 1992, that ratio had risen to one in three. During the same 10-year period, the white percentage of unwed mothers doubled, from 7.1 percent to 16.1 percent, while the nonwhite percentage rose from 47.8 percent to 63.7 percent.

Now, one out of every four children born in North Carolina (34,000 in 1994) is born to an unwed mother, locked almost always in a vicious cycle of poverty. The problem of illegitimacy has reached almost a crisis magnitude. Social scientists predict that unless this trend is reversed, by the year 2000, 40 percent of all American births and 80 percent of all minority births will be out-of-wedlock. Such a reality presents a frightening array of choices for our society. First, such explosive growth of the underclass which cannot support itself, would further burden, probably fatally, our fragile economy. Second, the implications of this population explosion among the underclass has dire implications for our already crippled justice system. Third, the reluctance of the government to make meaningful progress in solving this problem is demoralizing for hard-working taxpayers, who are becoming increasingly resentful of wasteful and ineffective social welfare spending programs. One result is a growing underground economy which leads to a decline in government revenue.

In spite of the trillions of dollars which have been spent in this country in the past quarter century toward the worthwhile goal of eliminating poverty and reducing the misery of America's afflicted, there is mounting evidence that the government's gallant efforts in the war on poverty have failed.

Our compassion for the unfortunate among us is truly one of the great attributes that sets Americans apart from and above many other citizens of the civilized world. However, something is out of balance when the portion of our State budget devoted to public assistance exceeds one-third of the total budget and is the fastest growing part of the budget. We must get control of this problem and solve the underlying causes of poverty before it consumes our civilized society. What we seem to be doing now is merely treating the symptoms of poverty and ignorance and not doing that very effectively.

Transportation

Transportation commanded $1.7 billion of the State budget in fiscal 1994 and, without question, the task of building a system of modern highways is an essential and worthwhile role for the State to play. The money we've spent to build and maintain North Carolina's 77,000 miles of State-maintained roads can be counted among our best and wisest public expenditures, because those expenditures have led directly to better jobs, a stronger economy, a vibrant and prosperous travel and tourism industry, and a higher quality of life for our own citizens.

The development of good roads was a precursor of the great strides forward in our State's economic base and stimulated North Carolina's transition from an agrarian economy to a great center of manufacturing and commerce. First in the 1840s, with the development of the railroad, and again in the 1920s, with the first Statewide initiative to build and maintain public highways for Mr. Ford's affordable Model T, the State broke new ground in its effort to stimulate economic growth by means of a better transportation system. Both the railroad and the new highways enabled farmers to get their crops to market quicker and surer. The State's system of modern interstate highways, begun in the 1960s, has become an essential part of our transportation network.

Because of the State's great size, geographical diversity and rural nature, transportation has been a great concern from the days of the earliest settlers, who first found little more than a meager system of Indian trails stretching across the great spans of wilderness as the civilization spread westward. In colonial times waterways were the primary avenues of commerce. Primitive dirt roads, some of them built by private entrepreneurs and operated by toll fees, began to spring up in early 1800s and these were replaced by plank roads which soon gave way to the mighty rail.

Railroads surged in the years just before the Civil War and again after Reconstruction. During Reconstruction millions of dollars in State bonds were fraudulently issued to build railroads; however, these bonds were repudiated later and future growth of the rail system became largely the responsibility of private investors.

The first early financial commitment to a public highway system came in 1921, when the General Assembly authorized the State to take over

5,500 miles of county roads. To pay for this, citizens approved a $50 million State highway bond issue, a motor fuel tax of one cent per gallon was imposed and a system of motor vehicle license and registration fees was established. Proceeds from the bond issue were used to build a system of hard-surfaced roads, connecting each of the State's 100 county seats. Enthusiasm for the roadbuilding program grew, and with it the demand for more public funds. The gas tax was increased to five cents a gallon and an additional $65 million issue of highway bonds was approved, bringing the total road building program to $115 million between 1921 and 1927. It was during this period that North Carolina earned title to "The Good Roads State."

Highway expansion came to an abrupt halt in 1931, as the ill effects of the Great Depression curtailed tax revenue. The General Assembly reacted by assuming responsibility for the construction and maintenance of all county roads. During the depression years, and through World War II, highway funds were diverted to other State programs–the General Fund, operation of the prison system and grants to cities, among others. The raid on the highway fund became so great that the General Assembly, in 1947, prohibited further diversions.

In 1949, during the administration of Governor W. Kerr Scott, the General Assembly put another bond issue before the voters, this time for a $200 million road building program, and at the same time raised the gas tax to seven cents a gallon. This was a very ambitious initiative since the proposed highway building program exceeded the annual budget of the State at that time. Some 15,000 miles of secondary roads were paved and an additional 15,000 of farm-to-market roads were stabilized.

By 1969, most of the 1949 debt had been repaid and a new $300 million bond issue was approved. In 1969, during the administration of Kerr Scott's son, Bob, the gasoline tax was increased to nine cents a gallon. Another $300 million highway bond issue was approved in 1977, and the motor fuel tax was increased to 12 cents in 1981. Again in 1986, the motor fuel tax was raised by the equivalent of three and one-half cents.

Almost one-third ($522 million) of the budget of the Department of Transportation (DOT) in fiscal 1994 came from the federal matching funds for improvements and construction on the State's primary and interstate highways. The Department employs 13,800 people, an average of one employee for every six miles of public highway in North Carolina, and is responsible for all modes of travel except for the State Ports, which

Table 6-2. History of the Gasoline Tax in North Carolina*

Year	Tax Increase	Total Tax
1909	1/2 cent per gallon	tax levied as inspection fee
1917	-1/4 cent per gallon	tax reduction to 1/4 cent/gal)
1921	1 cent per gallon	motor fuels tax (in addition to inspection fee)
1923	2 cents per gallon	3 cents
1925	1 cent per gallon	4 cents
1927		refunds allowed for nonhighway use
1929	1 cent per gallon	5 cents
1931	1 cent per gallon	6 cents
1950	1 cent per gallon	7 cents
1969	2 cents per gallon	9 cents
1981	3 cents per gallon	12 cents
1986	3.5 cents per gallon*	15.5 cents
1992	*	17.5 cents
1994	*	21.3 cents

*Effective July 15, 1986 the tax rate was changed to be set semiannually and based on a flat rate of 14 cents per gallon plus a percentage of the average wholesale price of gasoline. In 1989 the flat rate was increased to 17 cents per gallon and raised again in 1992 to 17.5 cents.

Note: This is in addition to the federal gasoline tax of 20.1 cents per gallon and 24.1 cents for diesel.

are operated by the Department of Commerce. DOT's two largest divisions are the Division of Highways, which builds and maintains the State road system, and the Division of Motor Vehicles, which is responsible for registering all motor vehicles and issuing drivers' licenses to qualified drivers. This division also certifies school bus drivers, collects traffic accident data, administers the International Registration Plan for trucks, and enforces motor carrier laws.

Because roads are so important to our State's economy and the fact that they touch every corner of the State by tying remote mountain and coastal communities to the urban, affluent piedmont, the Department of Transportation has been traditionally the most politically sensitive State agency. Members of the powerful Board of Transportation generally have been big campaign contributors to the Governor and seldom bring a global perspective to the Board. More often, they come with a predetermined list of priorities favoring the particular geographical area which they represent. Take for example, construction of the magnificent Faircloth Freeway, built to bypass the small town of Clinton in rural, sparsely populated Sampson County. Clinton did not have a pressing need for a bypass, though at that time U.S. Highways 421 and 701 were busy beach corridors in the summertime. What the town of Clinton did have, that was more persuasive than the critical highway needs of all five of the State's major urban centers, was a native son, Lauch Faircloth, sitting as Chairman of the North Carolina Board of Transportation when the decision was made to fund this dubious project. Democratic leaders found Faircloth's parochial greed an amusing diversion. Citizens of the densely populated Charlotte Metro area, who found themselves twice a day in highly congested traffic, negotiating their way to work and back home at a snail's pace, were not amused. Since Faircloth's defection to the Republican Party and defeat of an incumbent Democratic U.S. Senator, the story of how the Faircloth Freeway came to be built is remembered with less affection.

While roads, even secondary roads into the remote backways of rural North Carolina, are highly visible and the subject of constant vigilance by motorists who will complain at the slightest bump or pothole, the deterioration of the State's 14,000 bridges has become a major problem facing highway planners. Unlike an open highway whose surface reflects its current status, the major strength factors and other indicators of the condition of a bridge are hidden and must be inspected by trained engineers. Even when engineers report widespread and growing problems with our bridges, it is easy for the General Assembly to delay expensive maintenance and rebuilding decisions because of inadequate funding. A preliminary study in 1994 found that more than half the State's bridges were inadequate and in need of either repair or replacement, at a projected total cost of hundreds of millions of dollars.

With a huge bureaucracy in Raleigh and local offices in each of North Carolina's 100 counties, the Department of Transportation has been the target of frequent criticism, some of it deserved, for political patronage appointments, cronyism and mismanagement. In 1972, a new appointee of Governor Jim Holshouser, the first Republican elected governor in this century, was driving from Western North Carolina to his first meeting of the Board of Transportation. He saw a DOT truck parked along the road he was traveling and decided to stop and get acquainted. He found several employees engaged in idle gossip and asked them what they were doing. "Putting in eight," the leader of the crew said. Subsequent discussion of this incident by the Board and coverage by the State's major newspapers prompted a minor, short-lived effort to make the department more efficient. Holshouser had aided his upset victory by focusing on DOT's ineptness.

DOT has seen its share of scandals in recent years, eclipsing all the rest of State government agencies combined for malfeasance. In the 1960s, a popular Raleigh developer was convicted of bribing DOT officials to use paint from a company he represented on highway signs. He went to prison. In the mid-1980s, several prominent contractors were caught in a bid-rigging scheme which had flourished for several years. They pleaded guilty, made token restitution, and went to jail. A female employee was accused of selling sexual favors to co-workers in a basement storage room of the Division of Motor Vehicles in the late 1980s and another worker was found fixing revoked drivers' licenses for a fee.

Perhaps that is why the Department has found it necessary to assemble a 15-person public affairs staff and spend $700,000 a year striving to convince Tar Heel taxpayers that their Department of Transportation is doing a good job. To justify their existence in the 1995 budget, the flacks said they planned to issue 500 press releases, prepare one periodic report, conduct 20 ceremonies and hand out 160 awards and certificates.

DOT, among its thousands of busy workers, has a legal staff of 20 with a budget of more than $1 million, a civil rights office with 10 people and a budget of nearly a half million dollars annually, and a five-person staff to promote bicycle travel.

The Department of Transportation operates the Ferry System, providing transportation between North Carolina's beautiful and scenic but remote and isolated Outer Banks and the mainland.

Highway Trust Fund

In 1987, the General Assembly created the Highway Trust Fund and raised the gasoline tax 5.2 cents per gallon. In addition, motor vehicle registration and titling fees were raised. Although voters were promised that proceeds from the Highway Trust Fund would be used exclusively for highway construction purposes, there have been numerous diversions from the true concept of the highway fund as originally created by the General

Assembly. The most extensive of these actions was a $170 million transfer to the General Fund in 1993 and annually thereafter.

The rail program was given $400,000 from the Highway Trust Fund each year of the 1993-95 biennium for rail access to industrial plants ($200,000) and for rail inspections ($190,000). Public transit tapped the Highway Trust Fund for another $10 million each year. The proposed Global TransPark took $9 million from the Highway Trust Fund during the 1991-93 biennium. A $5 million reserve, ostensibly to buy a Raleigh-Durham to London route for American Airlines, was appropriated from the Trust Fund in 1993-94. Later, this appropriation was used to fund an international tourism marketing program, promoting North Carolina as a destination for European vacationers.

Justice

We spent $1.3 billion underwriting North Carolina's justice system in fiscal 1993-94. Nearly half of this amount was consumed just to operate our capacity-filled prison system. Providing for the public safety has been a matter of public necessity from the first days of the republic and it will always be a vital duty. However, something is out of balance with our sense of public purpose when, as a society, we are willing to spend more to lock up a person in a solitary prison cell, feed him and secure him, than it would cost to send him for the same period of time to the most expensive private university in North Carolina.

The Department of Correction, whose primary job is to operate North Carolina's prisons and secure some 21,000 inmates, has been the subject of much attention in recent years because of the lack of adequate space to lock up violent criminals, who instead are being released on early parole. The department employs 12,800 workers, which means its ratio of inmates to workers is 1.6:1. While the North Carolina prison system constantly finds all of its 21,000 beds filled, an additional 30,000 persons are convicted each year and sentenced to active prison time. To make room for the most heinous of these new arrivals, other offenders are released back into society, where most of them are soon in trouble again, often after harming innocent citizens.

The problem of crime and its escalating harm upon our civilized society grew to such a crisis in the spring of 1994 that Governor Jim Hunt called a special session of the General Assembly to deal with the issues. Legislative leaders first predicted the session would last only two weeks, but it dragged on for nearly two months. The primary consequence of the session was the spending of more than a quarter of a billion dollars annually essentially for more of the same kinds of programs which were not working very well in the first place.

The $27,000 annual cost per inmate that is spent to secure and maintain each inmate in our North Carolina prison system is an alarmingly high expense which could better be used elsewhere. For example, for that same amount of money you could add an additional teacher who would teach 150 students in our public schools, or send four students to any public university in the State for an entire year. Or you could send a student to Duke University, our most expensive private university, for what it costs to incarcerate a single prison inmate.

Again, the failure of our education system, coupled with many social problems, is impacting directly on the rising costs of our justice system. Nine out of ten prison inmates are high school dropouts. It is reasonable to assume that if we can reduce the number of students who drop out of school before they get at least a high school diploma, we can reduce our prison population. The problem of substance abuse, stemming from excessive use of alcohol and addictive drugs (primarily cocaine and heroin) is a major underlying cause of crime, leading to overcrowding prisons. Yet, we are having little success in addressing this issue.

The savings for each person who is prevented from becoming a prison inmate and instead becomes a productive citizen, earning a decent wage and paying his share of the costs of public services represents an enormous potential impact upon our system of public finance. For example, a productive worker, earning $20,000 is a $20,000 asset to our society as compared with the typical prison inmate who is a $27,000-a-year liability. That is a net difference of $50,000 a year. Multiply that figure by the 30,000 plus people we incarcerate and then you can see the total impact of crime upon our system of public finance. When you take into consideration that we need twice as many prison beds as now exist, the problem of crime takes on a crisis magnitude.

Government Performance Audit Commission

In 1993, the Government Performance Audit Commission (GPAC) recommended abolishing the entire Department of Crime Control and Public Safety, which acts as a headquarters for the Highway Patrol, National Guard, Emergency Preparedness, and a few other agencies, and transferring these agencies into other departments. This recommendation brought a chorus of howls from State government workers who saw their jobs threatened. Instead of eliminating the department, or even trimming it to make it more efficient, the General Assembly added more people and more work to its assigned tasks.

When the General Assembly convened in 1994 for its "short" budget session, the recommendations of GPAC from the previous year were hardly mentioned.

Environment, Health, and Natural Resources

The Department of Environment, Health, and Natural Resources spent almost a half billion dollars in 1994, half of it federal money, to prevent pollution and punish polluters, conserve our forests, operate our State Parks and a State zoo, conserve our valuable coastal and inland water resources, and protect the public health of our citizens. To achieve these worthwhile goals, the department and its various divisions employed 3,800 people.

General Government

It costs some $300 million to operate the multitude of state government agencies which perform a variety of duties, all purportedly in pursuit of the public purpose. These range from the small nuclear staff of the Governor's office to the sprawling Department of Administration with thousands of employees.

Commerce

The North Carolina Department of Commerce had a deceptively high budget of $252 million in 1994; however, most of those funds pass through Commerce into autonomous agencies such as the Employment Security Commission, which dispenses federally funded unemployment checks and deals with other employment issues; the Utilities Commission, which regulates telephone, electricity, private water companies and other utility rates, the Burial Commission and the Cemetery Commission, which together see that the recently departed from among us get a fair deal in their final transactions. Here, too, in Commerce is the Banking Commission, Savings Institutions Division, and Credit Union Divisions, each of which deal with a different area of regulating financial institutions. Also located in the Department is the Division of Community Assistance, which dispenses housing and development grants, mostly from federal sources, to local communities. MCNC, formerly known as the Microelectronic Center of North Carolina, was established to attract high-tech jobs to North Carolina and is a $34 million a year enterprise ($16 million from State funds) under Commerce, as is the Biotechnology Center, a similar high-tech initiative that fosters research and development technology which includes genetic engineering. It has a budget of $7 million.

The main mission of the Department of Commerce is to promote economic development by stimulating business activity and the creation of new jobs. It does this by aggressively courting new industries to locate facilities in North Carolina and encouraging existing industries to expand. The annual cost for this enterprise is $8 million. A major activity within Commerce, since the mid-1970s, has been the State's successful promotion of its travel industry, positioning North Carolina as a destination for leisure travelers and, in recent years, a growing destination for conventioneers. More than $7 million was budgeted in fiscal 1994 for the State's travel promotion and marketing efforts, a contributing factor in North Carolina's prosperous $8 billion annual tourism industry.

The North Carolina Film Office spends nearly a half million dollars a year recruiting film companies to use North Carolina locations for filming motion picture and television productions, both promoting our State as well as boasting our economy.

The State's executive aircraft operation is assigned to the Department of Commerce for budgeting and administrative purposes, though the aircraft are frequently used by the Governor, Lieutenant Governor, and other top State officials. When the aircraft are not being used to ferry top State officials around, they are available for the economic development program. Lauch Faircloth caught a great deal of flak from the news media when he was Secretary of Commerce for his frequent use of the State helicopter. In 1984, the Republican Party sued Governor Jim Hunt for allegedly using the State aircraft for political trips and he was forced to repay the State from his campaign funds a significant sum. While that move was in the best interest of North Carolina taxpayers, it inconvenienced the Republican administration of Governor Jim Martin during the next eight years and kept Republicans from using the State aircraft as frequently as they would have liked to do.

To operate the State's two executive aircraft which consisted in 1994 of a helicopter that will carry six people, fewer comfortably, and two fixed wing planes, the State budgets $1 million annually.

During his upset victory in 1964, Governor Dan Moore campaigned on the promise that, if elected, he would sell the State airplane, which he thought extravagant. Shortly after his inauguration Governor Moore kept his promise and ordered the aging DC-3, once owned by Arthur Godfrey, sold. Later Governor Moore admitted he was mistaken to suggest that the Governor of a great and large State such as North Carolina should not have access to executive air service. The old airplane was soon replaced by a larger, modern and more expensive jet.

Administration

The Department of Administration is a $95 million a year operation which oversees the various administrative functions of State government, including construction and planning. It maintains State buildings and provides landscaping, and janitorial service. Landscaping State grounds, for example, costs nearly $1 million a year.

A multitude of commissions and councils have been stashed away in the Department of Administration, apparently for lack of a better place to send them. For example, the Human Relations Council, with an annual budget of $650,000; the Rape Crisis Program, ($580,000); the North Carolina Council for Women, ($494,000); Domestic Violence Center and Program, ($2 million); and the Youth Involvement Office, ($448,000).

The State spends $44,000 a year maintaining the Ethics Board, whose only job is to see that State executives and appointees to the various State boards and commissions do not use their officials status for personal benefit. It costs $2 million a year for the State to maintain its capital police force and $4 million to operate the purchase and contract division, whose main duty is to see that hundreds of procurement regulations are obeyed in the purchase of hundreds of millions of dollars worth of goods and services each year.

The State of North Carolina is also a major tenant. In 1994, through its State Property Office, the State leased a total of 3.1 million square feet of property at an annual cost to taxpayers of $26.3 million.

Other

The Department of Cultural Resources spends nearly $51 million a year protecting, preserving and presenting our heritage, and promoting the arts. The task of collecting taxes owed the state is done well by the Department of Revenue, at an annual cost of $59 million. The Treasurer's Office spends $7 million managing public funds, the State Controller spends $10 million accounting for the public funds, and the State Auditor spends $9 million making sure that State funds are spent for the purpose for which they were authorized.

The Department of Labor spends $20 million to see that laws enacted to protect workers are obeyed.

The Department of Insurance spends $25 million a year making sure that insurance companies treat their North Carolina customers fairly.

The Department of Agriculture spends $70 million to promote North Carolina's important farm economy, which generates $5.1 billion in cash income annually, largely from the sale of tobacco, cotton, peanuts and various other grain crops, poultry, beef and hogs.

Summary

North Carolina leaders have been progressive over the years in committing public funds to education, highways, health care and the welfare of the State's citizens. However, now in the twilight of the 20th Century, we must take a cautious look at our spending practices.

A most alarming fact is that the number of tax recipients is growing at a much faster rate than the number of taxpayers. Public spending programs must be reviewed more aggressively to make sure they are restricted to necessary and useful public purposes and that funds are being used prudently. Anything less than this will hasten a taxpayer revolt here such as which has occurred elsewhere in the nation in recent years.

Chapter 7

The General Assembly's Role in Budgeting

With its perceived unrestrained power to tax and spend, the General Assembly is sovereign in its ability to take from its citizens their labor and wealth and redistribute these resources as it sees fit. But even that awesome power is temporary because the citizens have the power every two years to elect a new General Assembly which more closely reflects their priorities.

In North Carolina, the only State in America in which the Governor does not have veto power, the General Assembly has final say in all legislative matters. Its power to levy taxes and choose where those taxes will be spent has the greatest impact upon the individual taxpayer of any of the numerous powers exercised by the General Assembly. Its power of the public purse is also its most awesome tool in setting policy for the destiny of the State.

Until the mid-1980s, most of the real power of the General Assembly to enact the State's budget resided in the hands of no more than a half dozen of the most powerful leaders of both houses. When the Lieutenant Governor, President Pro Tempore of the Senate, the Speaker of the House and the Chairs of the Appropriations and Finance Committees in both houses agreed on the budget, that was pretty much the end of discussion. The matter was settled.

Committee chairs and leadership in the General Assembly are based pretty much on seniority and a member's relationship with the top leadership. Traditionally, most senior members have come from rural areas, which has resulted in most of the key leadership positions being held by representatives of the more sparsely populated, rural regions of the State. Until the 1960s a small group of powerful eastern and western North Carolina legislators dominated the General Assembly because of their seniority and because of the reluctance of those in power to realign legislative districts so as to fairly represent the more populous piedmont. It took a Supreme Court order in the mid-1960s to force the General Assembly to restructure district boundaries so that all citizens of the State are represented equally. Since that court decision, urban areas have had equal representation, in terms of numbers; however, urban representatives in the North Carolina General Assembly seldom have been able to attain the seniority and power which rural members have enjoyed.

Former Governor Robert W. Scott recalls the days when his Uncle Ralph Scott, a State Senator, and father, the late Kerr Scott, one of North Carolina's most colorful and energetic Governors, would sit at the kitchen table of their farm home in Alamance County along with one or two other legislators and "mark up the budget," as they called the procedure. The budget-making process today has become more complicated, with lengthy budget appropriation hearings ensuring input from more legislators. Still, the major decisions relating to the power over the public purse in North Carolina are controlled by just a few of the 170 members of the General Assembly.

The Budget Process

The budget bill can originate in either House. Traditionally, the House and Senate take turns initiating the basic budget documents. Then, the other house takes that bill and adds its touch, usually offering many variances in appropriation priorities. After months of debate, major differences inevitably exist between the House and Senate budget bills and not until these are reconciled through a joint conference committee can there be a State budget. The budget proposal, like all prospective legislation, is called a bill during the deliberative process. Only when it is finally approved by a majority of both the House of Representatives and the Senate, does it become an act.

Preparation of the budget begins with the Governor, who is charged by the State Constitution to "prepare and recommend to the General Assembly a comprehensive budget of the anticipated revenues and proposed expenditures of the State for the ensuing fiscal period." When the Governor's budget, usually a cumbersome document of more than a thousand pages detailing the funding requests for every existing and newly proposed State government program, is submitted to the General Assembly it is merely a recommendation. "The Governor proposes, the General Assembly disposes," according to an old adage.

What emerges after months of hearings and days of backroom maneuvering is a compromise between what many want to be done and what is to be done. Seldom does the Governor or any of the various special interest groups get all they want out of a proposed budget. There is never enough money to go around. When members of the General Assembly begin to consider the complex budget requests, each legislator will attempt to make his or her own mark by funding pet projects they support and reducing ones they don't like.

The Budget

The North Carolina State budget is organized into three major parts: the continuation budget, the expansion budget, and the capital improvements budget. The continuation budget provides for continuing existing programs, meaning that unless special action is taken to eliminate or reduce an ongoing program, its funding level most likely will remain the same as for the previous year. The expansion budget provides for increases to existing programs or new programs. The capital improvements budget provides for construction, major repairs, and land purchases.

Of these, the continuation budget accounts for, by far, the largest outlay—usually 90 percent or more of the total budget. Little scrutiny has been given to the continuation budget in recent years, an inherent weakness in the State's budgeting process. Acting upon the assumption that existing programs are necessary and worthwhile, otherwise they would not have been approved in the first place, legislative leaders have spent very little time examining the value of ongoing programs. This policy has resulted in the rapid growth of State government in recent years, as many new programs were added to existing ones, funded by the rapid and steady increases in North Carolina's vibrant economy during the late 1970s and early 1980s. Growth in the tax base resulted in expanding revenues by an average of nearly $400 million per year, without a major tax increase. That trend stopped abruptly with the economic slowdown in 1988-89 and resulted in the most serious budget crisis which the State had faced since the Great Depression, some 60 years earlier. For the first time in many years, the General Assembly spent considerable time and effort during its 1993 session examining the continuation budget, searching for ways in which existing programs could be reduced or made more effective. While the General Assembly did not actually make many cutbacks, it did slow the rate of increased spending. This scenario and the likelihood that North Carolina's tax base will not grow as fast in the future as it has in the past, signals a strong possibility that the continuation budget will get more scrutiny in the future as it should.

Revenue Sources

Four major sources of revenue provide funds for these expenditures: the General Fund (56 percent), the Highway Fund (9.9 percent), federal

Figure 7-1. State Budget by Source, Fiscal Year 1993-94

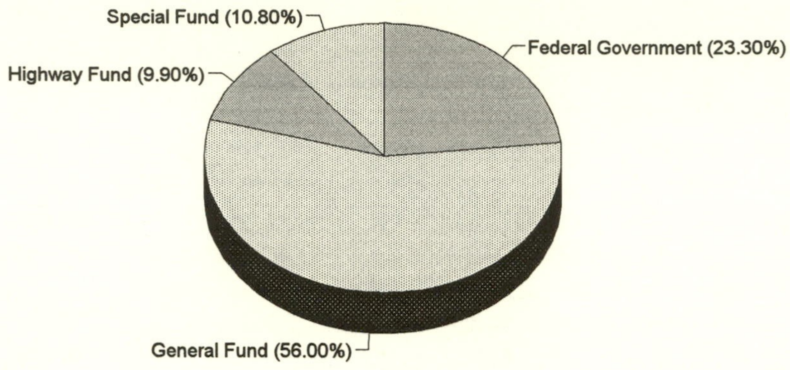

funds (23.3 percent) and special revenue funds (10.8 percent). The General Fund derives its revenue from such sources as the sales tax, individual and corporate income taxes and the franchise tax. In addition, the General Fund includes revenue from a number of nontax sources such as earnings from the Treasurer's investments, fees from the State courts and a variety of fees charged for State services. The sales tax, and individual and corporate income taxes typically account for about 85 percent of the General Fund's tax revenues.

The Highway Fund consists of revenues from transportation activities, primarily the gasoline taxes, motor vehicle registration fees, and drivers license fees. In 1987, the Highway Fund was divided into two parts. Upon the enactment of new gasoline taxes earmarked for a massive new highway building program, this new program was called the Highway Trust Fund and revenues were earmarked for that purpose.

Special Funds

Special revenue funds usually make up less than 10 percent of the total budget and include the receipts from such activities as the Wildlife Resources Commissions, university auxiliary services, motor pools, State Fair, prison enterprises and regulatory agencies, and general services.

Federal Funds

Federal funds account for a huge portion of the North Carolina budget. In fiscal 1994, for example, the State budget included $4.5 billion in federal funds. There has been a dramatic increase in both the amount and in the proportionate share of federal dollars in the State budget during the past three decades. For example, in 1965 the State budget included $153 million or 17 percent of the total. By 1994, the federal portion of the State budget had increased to 27 percent of the total.

Programs receiving the most federal funds are Medicaid, Aid to Families with Dependent Children, public schools, higher education and highway construction.

Revenue Estimates

Probably the most important part of the General Assembly's budget making process is its attempt to forecast future revenues. Since the North Carolina Constitution requires a balanced operating budget, actual expenditures cannot exceed actual revenues. Before it can authorize expenditures, the legislature must decide how much it has available to spend. Initial revenue forecasts are developed by the General Assembly's fiscal research staff, which includes experienced economists and technical analysts. They take into consideration every conceivable factor which is likely to affect the State's economy for the next two years. Factors like the vigor of the national economy, the likely impact of new tax policies, status of reserve funds, weather, and even the potential of war are also weighed.

The Governor also has his own team of revenue forecasters who, working independently of the General Assembly's experts, attempt to reach their own estimate of just how much revenue the State's economy and tax structure will produce. This process worked well for North Carolina until 1989 because of double-digit revenue growth and large reversions of unspent appropriations. In order to fund their extensive new spending programs that year, leaders of the General Assembly indulged in a game of upmanship with the Governor in the matter of forecasting future revenue. Ultimately, the General Assembly accepted the overly optimistic revenue forecast of the Governor's budget experts–a decision which its leaders came to regret during the spring of 1990, when the State approached the end of the fiscal year with revenue nearly a half billion dollars less than what had been projected. Almost all of the energy of the General Assembly during its 1991 session was spent looking for ways to cut the proposed new budget, and trying to find the least painful way to close a potential $1.3 billion gap between needed expenditures and projected revenues.

New revenue was found through a combination of increasing the sales tax and the corporate income tax, and raising a variety of "user" fees. Total cuts in proposed spending amounted to more than $600 million and new taxes generated more than $600 million. Although some members of the General Assembly later campaigned for re-election by saying they had voted to cut State government spending during 1991, that was not quite true. They only had voted to slow down the rate of new spending. As a result of the budget changes and increased taxes enacted during the 1991 session, State revenues increased by nearly a billion dollars the following year.

If the revenues which are forecast do not materialize, the Governor, as administrator of the budget, is required by law to cut back spending to the actual levels of current revenues. The Treasurer has an important constitutional duty in this process, because it is his responsibility, by law, also to see that the State's outlays do not exceed its revenues. In the event that the executive branch attempts to spend more money than the State has on hand, it would be the Treasurer's duty to refuse to authorize such deficit spending, that the federal government does routinely and recklessly. Though it has never been necessary to use that authority in North Carolina, its very existence gives confidence in our fiscal responsibility and is one of the reasons why our State has maintained a Triple-A credit rating since the 1960s.

Developing the Budget

North Carolina's fiscal year runs from July 1 to June 30 and the State budget is organized accordingly. The budget-making process is a year-long and continuing task for State agencies. Because members of the General Assembly are elected for two years, they approve a biennial budget during the main or "long" session which is scheduled in odd numbered years. There is no legal prohibition against adoption of annual budgets, if the legislators were to choose to do so. Since 1974, the General Assembly has held a "short" session in even-numbered years, primarily for the purpose of reviewing revenue projections and refining the budget during the second year of the biennium.

Approximately a year before the regular "long" session of the General Assembly is to begin during odd-numbered years, the Office of Budget and Management issues instructions to State departments and agencies for making biennial requests for each component of the budget—continuation, expansion and capital. These instructions include schedules for submission, forms to be used, allowable price and inflationary rate increases and requirements for supporting schedules. The Office of Budget and Management also distributes information on demographic, economic and inflationary trends, on the implications of court decisions, federal legislation, and other relevant factors which need to be considered in preparing the budget requests.

Budget requests from each agency are accompanied by a statement of each program's goals, its objectives for the next two years, statistical data supporting its objectives, the actual line-item budget for the current year and the recommended line-item budget requested or recommended for the next two years. Agencies are given about six months to prepare their request. During this process agency administrators, every one of which thinks his or her program is the most important program in all of State government, compete to see that their requests stay alive. The Cabinet Secretary of each department, in consultation with the Governor, decides the level of requests for the continuation and expansion budgets, and his priority for those requests will be submitted to the Office of State Budget and Management which conducts its review of all agency requests and, in the fall of even numbered years, prepares the Governor's recommended budget. Elected Council of State members also submit their priority requests to the Office of Budget and Management, hoping their recommendations will be included in the Governor's budget.

Advisory Budget Commission

The Governor is assisted in preparing the budget by the 15-member Advisory Budget Commission (ABC) which is created by statute and consists of five senators appointed by the President Pro Tempore of the Senate, five representatives appointed by the Speaker of the House and five members appointed by the Governor. While the role of the Advisory Budget Commission is now advisory, as its name implies, it once held enormous power when the General Assembly was not in session. The ABC exercised almost total power over budget matters until the Supreme Court ruled that such interference into the executive branch by the legislature was unconstitutional. Members of the legislature still serve on a number of commissions and councils which influence various agencies within the executive branch; however, all of these commissions and councils are advisory rather than administrative or regulatory.

The Budget Bill In The General Assembly

In each House, there is an Appropriations Committee and a Finance Committee. Both the Speaker of the House and the President Pro Tempore of the Senate appoint about half of the members of each body to the respective Appropriations Committee and the other half to the Finance Committee. The Appropriations Committee considers how the money will be spent. The Finance Committee considers where the money will come from, including whether any tax increase is needed.

An assignment on the Appropriations Committee is considered a choice assignment because that is where a legislator can influence which programs get funding. It is less fun to be a member of the Finance Committee because there the legislator has to make tough decisions about sources of new revenue. It is much easier to run for re-election citing support for a popular new program which you helped fund than to defend the act of raising taxes. Theoretically, reducing taxes is another option, though not one frequently chosen.

The huge Appropriations Committee is subdivided into smaller committees which look at the various programs of government–Education, General Government, Human Resources, Justice and Public Safety, and Natural Resources. Separate committees consider the continuation, expansion and capital budgets.

Agency heads are summoned before the various legislative committees to explain their programs and justify their requests for more money. In addition, experts from the legislature's fiscal research staff are called upon to explain their perspectives about proposed programs. Unless a program has gained notoriety through gross mismanagement or has been singled out by the media or a powerful special interest group, these hearings are fairly routine. Seldom have existing programs been cut. However, due to limited resources, increased competition for expansion funding and new programs, the General Assembly will have to scrutinize the continuation budget more carefully in the future. There is a growing concern among leading officials that State government has grown too large in recent years and deserves a critical review to make sure all programs are serving the "public purpose" as dictated by the State Constitution.

In theory, the various committees listen to agency heads, concerned citizens, and others with special interests in continuing, expanding or creating new programs, and then decide what ought to be funded. The sub-committee reports its recommendations to the full Appropriations

Committee, which decides how to allocate the available funding.

In reality, the process works quite differently. Personalities of the key players, and their clout in the General Assembly, become a major factor in most funding decisions. During the 1993 session, for example, a powerful State Senator inserted a pet project in the Senate budget which generated widespread criticism in the press. It was the creation of a special judicial district in his sparsely populated region of the State which almost everyone in the district agreed was not needed. Although the judgeship was opposed by a majority of the House members and the Governor, it survived all efforts to delete it because of the persistence of Senate leaders. Ironically, members of the legislature found themselves back in Raleigh in a special session in February of 1994, called by Governor Jim Hunt to deal with a perceived crisis of increased crime.

There are dozens of incidents each legislative session involving pet projects pushed through by members of both houses for things of dubious value to the taxpayers. Take for example the numerous "visitor" centers which have sprung up around North Carolina. Many of these facilities, built inside the State, are promoted as a means of helping sell North Carolina to travelers who otherwise might drive on by. Several are built on roads seldom traveled by visitors. Others are located well inside North Carolina and serve primarily as a vehicle for dispensing brochures to visitors already here. One such center is even located on the outbound lanes of a four-lane highway near the Georgia border. It has been unaffectionately referred to as a "Farewell Center."

This type of funding "pet" projects for powerful legislators is criticized as "pork barrel" funding by the press and other members who don't have the influence to bring home the "bacon" for their districts.

Several years ago a high-ranking bureaucrat decided that the State ought to build a refinery to reprocess oil used in the State's automobile fleet. Millions of dollars were spent developing this scheme and selling it to the Governor, who persuaded the General Assembly that the State could save money by doing this. The refinery was built at a substantial cost of taxpayer dollars yet never saved the State a dime and was shut down a few years later after a huge waste. Was the bureaucrat who contrived this scheme disciplined? No, quite the contrary. She was promoted and continues to promote "savings" measures, co-sponsored by those who stand to benefit handsomely.

The "Super Sub"

The legislative budget-making process changed drastically in the late 1980s and early 1990s. For many years, final decisions on the budget were made by a tightly knit group of eight veteran legislators known as the "Super Sub." The official name for this group was the Budget Conference Committee and their role, as is the role for all conference committees, was to reconcile differences between the House and Senate versions of the budget bill. However, the "Super Sub" gained a well-deserved reputation for being secretive, arbitrary, capricious and at times arrogant in the discharge of their most important duty. Few members outside the "Super Sub" except for perhaps the Speaker of House and the Lieutenant Governor, understood many of the budget bill's implications until after it had been enacted.

There is the well-told story of the "Super Sub's" particularly intense hearings during the early 1960s. Governor Terry Sanford had led the effort to extend the sales tax to food and for years afterwards several members of the General Assembly tried unsuccessfully to eliminate the "food tax." The chairman of the Senate Appropriations Committee had an understanding with a few of his subordinates how to signal to them the way they should vote. The signal, I was told, was that just before the vote, if he pulled his left ear, that meant the bill was bad and it should be voted down. If he pulled his right ear that was a signal to vote in the affirmative. On this one occasion, a couple of the committee members were sitting in the back of the room, carrying on their own discussion, when suddenly a vote was called.

Unaware as to how he should vote, the naive member stood up and said, "Mr. Chairman, I'm sorry, I missed your signal. I didn't see which ear you pulled. Would you take a minute and explain how we should vote?" After a few seconds of awkward silence, the committee room shook with laughter, as only a few members of the committee were aware how the chairman had been getting the word to his loyal followers. The chairman was not amused.

Frustrations reached a peak in January of 1989 and culminated with the overthrow of veteran House Speaker Liston Ramsey, who was defeated in his bid for re-election. A group of 21 "renegade" Democrats joined with the entire Republican House delegation to elect Representative Joe Mavretic of Edgecombe County as Speaker. Mavretic opened up the legislative process as he promised to do. The "Super Sub" was replaced by a more representative Conference Committee, which conducted its lengthy deliberations in public. Although Representative Mavretic was not re-elected Speaker in 1991, many of the open-door policies he instituted were followed by his successor.

The organization of Finance Committees is less extensive because only a few major new revenue bills are considered in any one session. Because of its complexity and sheer volume, the process of considering and adopting the budget is the most time consuming task that the General Assembly undertakes. And for this reason, the budget is usually the last matter resolved.

Government Performance Audit Commission

In December of 1992, the long-awaited recommendation of the Government Performance Audit Commission (GPAC) unveiled the results of its two-year long effort to reduce inefficiency and waste in North Carolina State government. The GPAC recommendations had been loudly touted by candidates for statewide and legislative races during the 1992 campaign as a genuine and sincere means of identifying wasteful and unnecessary programs. There was great anticipation among legislators, the press, and the public that GPAC would identify wasteful and unnecessary programs which could then be eliminated or improved, ostensibly to free up funds for more worthwhile public spending.

A total of 275 bills were introduced during the 1993 session of the General Assembly to implement the various GPAC recommendations. Supporters argued that these measures would save nearly $300 million in State expenditures. GPAC identified some 7,500 State jobs which could be eliminated. Yet, when forced to act, the General Assembly chose to cut fewer than a hundred positions and most of these cuts were made in a single agency, the Department of Public Instruction, already one of the smallest departments in State government. And, at the same time the General Assembly was cutting a few jobs in the Department of Public Instruction, it added hundreds of positions in other departments.

Of the original 275 GPAC bills, only five were adopted, at a projected savings of only $30 million in the first year of the biennium and $43 million during the second year of the biennium. The disappointing experience of the North Carolina General Assembly in dealing with a variety of rather modest recommendations to eliminate waste and inefficiency in State government illustrates the problem that all governments face today. Special interest groups, government employees, and legislators themselves form a strong and articulate constituency which resists all threats to the status quo, no matter how well deserved the proposed changes.

By 1994, when the General Assembly returned for its "short" budget session, the GPAC and its money-saving recommendations were all but forgotten.

Legislative Oversight

Since the 1975-77 biennium, the General Assembly has exercised its "continuing" oversight of the State budget through the Joint Legislative Commission on Governmental Operations. The commission has 22 members, consisting of nine members from the House and eight from the Senate. In addition, its ex-officio members include the Speaker and Speaker Pro Tempore of the House, the Lieutenant Governor, President Pro Tempore and majority leader of the Senate. The Commission's primary duty is to monitor State government operations during periods when the legislature is not in session, and assure that funds are being used for the purpose for which they were authorized. This Commission is becoming more powerful as it meets on a monthly basis. There is broad concern that this Commission in recent years has attempted to usurp authority reserved by the Constitution for the executive branch of State government.

Change Is Needed

Substantial change is needed in the budget process. During the past half century, our public leaders have become chained to the wagon of taxes and services. This was acceptable as long as tax revenues rose consistently, but when economic growth slowed and fiscal crises hit, the equation changed. The kind of government that developed during the industrial era, with sluggish, centralized bureaucracies, preoccupation with rules and regulations, and a hierarchical chain of command, no longer works very well. Our government has become bloated, wasteful and often ineffective. The world around us has changed much during the past two decades, yet government has failed to follow the changes and adapt accordingly.

When our State and nation's political parties were stronger they could resist strong pressures to increase spending by exercising control over members. Now that the political parties are weak and ineffective, legislators operate largely as individuals, raising their own campaign money and rising or falling on their own reputation and voting record. Hence there is little incentive for the legislative bodies to look beyond the short-term spending interests of their constituents. Many special interests have succeeded in electing their own advocates to the legislature and when they arrive, they make little effort to conceal the fact they are there to represent a narrow constituency and not all citizens.

Our traditional budget-making process encourages public managers to waste money. If managers don't spend their entire budget by the end of the fiscal year, three things happen: the money saved is taken away, less money is appropriated next year, and the budget director scolds them for requesting too much money in the first place. Hence, the time-honored government practice is to rush to spend all funds by the end of the fiscal year, including many needless and frivolous expenditures.

Instead of this wasteful practice, we should allow managers to keep a portion of their savings, using these funds in ways which make their programs more efficient and effective. We should go a step further, implementing efficiency measures which inspire managers to examine their programs and seek ways to provide necessary services more effectively, reducing or eliminating programs no longer needed.

In government, the budget is the most important control mechanism. By looking only at the spending side of the budget, and not at the outcome side of the ledger, much taxpayer money is wasted. For example, it is not in the public interest to postpone road repairs until the road has to be rebuilt at three times the cost of resurfacing.

There is much to be said for zero-based budgets which require that all programs be completely justified and re-funded each biennium. This would drastically change the process by which nearly 90 percent of North Carolina's budget is approved for re-funding each year now with only cursory attention. The practice of routinely funding existing programs through the continuation budget locks in many unnecessary programs which consume resources that would be better used elsewhere.

Many of our nation's innovative counties and cities have adopted radical new budget systems which allow managers to respond quickly as circumstances change. These systems eliminate line-item budgets and allow managers to shift resources around as needs shift. They also allow agencies to keep what they don't spend from one year to the next so unused funds can be allocated to new priorities. The only thing more destructive than a line-item budget is a personnel system built around civil service which protects mediocrity and inhibits creativity. In the business world, personnel is a support function, helping managers function more effectively. In traditional government, personnel is a control function.

We should give serious consideration to replacing our archaic line-item budgets with mission-driven budgets. Mission-driven budgets give employees an incentive to save money. Mission-driven budgets free up resources to test new ideas. Line-item budgets trap resources into old patterns. Those who rail against waste and abuse in government but defend the line-item budget process should think again. These rigid control systems make waste inevitable. Because they don't measure results, bureaucratic governments rarely achieve worthwhile accomplishments. Look, for example, at our troubled public schools. We have spent more and more on public schools in this State and throughout the nation, yet test scores and dropout rates barely change. We spend more and more on welfare and job training, yet welfare rolls continue to grow. We spend more and more on police and prisons, yet crime rates rise.

These are issues in which the General Assembly must take an expanded role in the future, because taxpayers are becoming concerned about the value they are getting for their tax dollars. In a republic, such as ours, the faith of our citizens in their government is essential. For the republic to survive, its citizens must have a strong sense of confidence in their elected public officials. Citizens must feel they can trust their public officials to spend public funds with great care and only for purposes that clearly are for the public good. When that faith is lost, the republic is doomed. Fortunately, our citizens have the power to redress grievances by replacing unfaithful public servants. That power has been exercised with increasing frequency in recent years and remains our best guarantee against tyranny.

We are approaching the point in this State and in this country when government officials at all levels—local, state and federal—must reassess the way they do business and make substantial changes in both the mission and operation of many public programs.

Chapter 8

Local Government In North Carolina

From ashes to excellence: The story of how local governments rose from disaster in the Great Depression to become the best managed in the nation.

Local governments provide most of the services used on a day-to-day basis by North Carolina citizens. Counties, acting as agents of State government, deliver services that apply to all citizens. Municipalities provide additional, proprietary-type services needed by people who live in urban areas. While they do it with revenue raised mostly at the state and federal levels, counties operate the public schools, administer justice, provide local law enforcement, distribute welfare payments, and provide an array of other social services. Municipalities take away the garbage and sewage, provide clean water and fire protection, regulate building codes, determine land-use policies, maintain law enforcement within their boundaries, and, in some cases, operate electric power and gas distribution systems for their constituents.

Combined county and municipal budgets in North Carolina totaled $8.8 billion in 1993, exceeding the State's General Fund. The cities and counties employed approximately 36,000 and 44,000 employees respectively. These totals do not include school personnel which add another State-funded but locally hired 131,000 professional and support employees to the payrolls of local government. In summary, local governments account for about half of the direct public expenditures within North Carolina and for more than two-thirds of the total State and local public employment.

This system of shared responsibility for raising revenue at the State level and delivering services at the local level evolved from the special needs of a widely dispersed population throughout a large State and was influenced significantly by the Great Depression. It has proven to be an effective and efficient method for providing essential public services. There has not been a single default of public debt by a local government entity in North Carolina since the Great Depression. In 1993, at a time when local governments all over the nation were struggling to balance their books, 25 percent of all the Triple-A rated state and local government units in the nation were in North Carolina. In 1992, North Carolina had 905 units of local governments and special tax districts–100 counties, 516 municipalities and 321 special fire districts, hospital districts, and sanitation, school and other special purpose tax districts. While the county is the major unit of government for administering statewide (education and social) services, each varies substantially in size. Chowan, in the northeast is only 172 square miles in size while Robeson, in the southcentral spans 949 square miles. Population varies, too, ranging from sparsely populated Tyrrell County (3,856) in the east to sprawling Mecklenburg (511,433) in the western piedmont, according to the 1990 census. In the decade since the previous census, the population of Tyrrell County had shrunk 119 people, while Mecklenburg's population had grown 107,000.

History of Local Government

North Carolina's system of government is a descendant of the kind of government established here during Colonial America when the county was the principal local government unit, formed to administer basic public services to a widely dispersed population. Since the Revolutionary War, when North Carolina's constitution gave supreme power to the General Assembly to make laws and set policy for all government within the State, counties have served essentially as agents of the State. Towns were slow to develop and when they did, were chartered as municipalities to provide additional services needed by people who lived in more populated areas.

Even today the General Assembly retains legal authority for all governmental operations. Counties and cities are permitted to act only with specific authority as granted by the General Assembly. The concept of "home rule" is severely restricted. While this may appear to be a cumbersome way to operate government in today's complex world, it has proven to be financially sound, practical and effective.

Prior to 1900 counties in North Carolina were responsible for financing and administering the basic governmental operations, including law enforcement, incarceration of most prisoners, operating ourts, public schools, roads, public health, and what meager efforts that were made to aid the poor. Municipal governments played only a minor role because there were so few of them. Property taxes accounted for most of the revenue raised at both the state and county levels.

The Great Depression

Much of the financial pain brought on by the Great Depression in the early 1930s was caused by the fact that local government officials did not foresee the risks which accompanied the boom period following World War I. Local debt in North Carolina increased seven-fold in the decade after the war, rising from less than $50 million in the early 1920s to more than $350 million in early 1931.

Much of this debt was brought on by the legitimate need for better roads and better schools. Some of it was inspired by an attractive bond market, spurred by tax exemptions for investors buying public debt. But it was also increased by unscrupulous bond salesmen and by the lack of statutory or constitutional controls to keep local officials from incurring imprudent public debt.

Local officials found themselves in deep financial trouble in 1931, as all economic indicators dropped sharply. Falling land values sent property taxes plummeting. By the end of 1930, delinquent property taxes in North Carolina exceeded $7.5 million and more than 150,000 pieces of property were being advertised for sale in order to satisfy tax liens.

Cash farm income dropped from $283 million in 1928 to $97 million in 1932. Value added by manufacture declined by more than one-third from a high of $603 million in 1929. There were 18 bank failures in North Carolina in 1929, and more than 200 bank failures in the next four years.

The counties responded in the only way possible. Budgets were slashed with a significant cutback in services. Salaries of teachers and public officials were reduced. Roads were neglected. Even with these drastic and unprecedented measures, local government officials were unable to pay their debts. **By 1933, 62 counties, 152 municipalities, and some 200 special tax districts were in default on bond payments. More local governments defaulted in North Carolina than in any other state.** It was indeed a troubled time for a state and its people struggling to survive.[32]

Three factors had contributed to these massive defaults. First, bonds had been issued haphazardly with little thought to repayment schedules. Inadequate provision had been made for principal payments due in the next decade. Second, while a "sinking fund" had been required by the State to provide for debt service, many local officials neglected to set funds aside on a regular basis for meeting the huge principal and interest

[32]Lefler and Newsome, *The History of a Southern State*, 572-577.

payments that would come due. And third, the depression resulted in a swift and significant decline in government revenues.

Faced with these overwhelming financial burdens, State leaders were assaulted with an avalanche of proposals. Farmers marched on the General Assembly demanding relief from ad valorem property taxes and suggested that the State's wealthy citizens bear an increased tax burden in the form of a "luxury tax." This was rejected. Instead, the General Assembly decided upon a bold course of action in 1931 and 1933 that drastically transformed the concept of State and local government in North Carolina.

North Carolina Reinvents Local Government

Out of the economic chaos of the Great Depression, a new state-local government relationship was born in North Carolina. During the fiscal revolution of 1931-33, the General Assembly decided that the State would assume responsibility for building and maintaining roads, for operating the public schools, and building and operating prisons.

To pay for these programs, statewide income taxes were increased and a sales tax was enacted. Before these changes, revenue to pay for schools, roads and prisons was raised primarily from local ad valorem taxes, which accounted for two-thirds of all State and local government revenue. After the changes, State revenue sources, primarily the income and sales taxes, accounted for two-thirds of all State and local government revenue. In doing this, North Carolina adopted a strong partnership with its local governments. Revenue would be raised in a centralized manner at the State level, but services would be delivered in a decentralized fashion by the counties.

There was one more very significant change. The General Assembly insisted on strict supervision of local government financial administration.

Local Government Commission

The 1931 General Assembly, in response to a plea from the Association of County Commissioners, created the Local Government Commission and gave it authority to review and approve all proposed bond and note issues by local governments. Furthermore, the Local Government Commission was given a mandate to enforce the sinking fund provisions which established a procedure for setting aside funds on a regular basis for bond interest and principal payments. Under the provisions of the 1931 legislation to put local governments back on a sound fiscal footing, sales of local government bonds and notes were to be made by the Commission. In the event of default, the Commission was given authority to intercede directly into the affairs of the troubled city or county, take financial control of the operation and levy additional taxes necessary to repay bondholders. While that provision has never been used, its mere existence has inspired responsible financial management by the State's local governments.

The Local Government Commission became an outgrowth of the County Government Advisory Commission, established by the General Assembly in 1927 to study the growing difficulties of local government in North Carolina and recommend a solution. Governor Angus W. McLean appointed Dr. E. C. Brooks, then president of State College, now N.C. State University, as chairman. Charles M. Johnson was the Advisory Commission's executive secretary. Johnson became State Treasurer in 1933, and served ably for 16 years, helping to lead North Carolina during the recovery from the Great Depression.

Also the 1927 General Assembly enacted five major pieces of legislation which became the foundation on which the County Government Advisory Commission (later the Local Government Commission) built the sound fiscal management system that exists today in North Carolina. Those acts resulted in establishment of the Advisory Commission the requirement that each county adopt an annual budget and spend no more money than appropriated in the budget. Also imposed were restrictions on the use of bonds and public indebtedness, limited authority to sell land and property for taxes, strengthened use of liens and foreclosures for delinquent taxes, and a provision for stiff penalties for tax delinquents.

One of the new provisions required each county to appoint a county accountant and stipulated that a uniform classification of accounts for counties be prepared. Uniform budgeting and bookkeeping forms were designed. A county calendar was prepared, outlining the duties of the various county officers and setting a date by which those duties were to be performed. A fiscal code for county officials was compiled by the Attorney General and published by the Commission.

During its four years of existence the County Government Advisory Commission moved boldly to establish sound fiscal practices for local government, but was handicapped in that its role was merely advisory. It had no power to order implementation of its policies. Furthermore, the Commission did not have adequate personnel to advise counties in resolving numerous inevitable defaults.

The General Assembly corrected these shortcomings by creating the Local Government Commission in 1931, with the Local Government Act. The new commission was given the mandate of restoring fiscal sanity to local government finance in North Carolina and it was given ample power to do the job. Its members included the State Treasurer, Secretary of State, State Auditor, Commissioner of Revenue, and six members to be appointed by the Governor. Charles M. Johnson was named the first Director of Local Government by Governor O. Max Gardner, and W. E. Easterling, a stalwart in his own right, was named assistant director.

Among the responsibilities given the Local Government Commission in 1931 were:

1. approval of all bonds and notes proposed for issuance by any local government;
2. sale of all bonds and notes;
3. strict accounting and safeguarding of all local funds, with particular attention to mandating and supervision of the sinking funds for the retirement of debt;
4. insuring prompt payment of principal and interest;
5. uniform accounting of local government finances;
6. mandating and supervising local government audits; and,
7. maintaining the integrity of local funds to keep public officers from intermingling public funds with their own funds.

The Local Government Commission faced two challenges. First, it had to find a way to assist local governments in paying down the enormous public debt that had accumulated during the Roaring Twenties, which reached a peak of $360 million in 1932. Second, it had to find a way to allow the financing of necessary capital improvements within the ability of local government to pay for such improvements. Both objectives have been achieved in such a commendable way that North Carolina's Local Government Commission has become the envy of local officials throughout much of the rest of the nation.

By 1946, total local bonded debt in North Carolina had been reduced to $241 million. Following World War II, local debt began to rise again; however, property values also began a steady increase, which resulted in growing revenue.

Local Government Today

Today, local governments in North Carolina are financially sound. In fact, our local governments have established a well-earned national reputation for being among the best managed and most fiscally responsible in all America. This recognition comes not only from half a century of stable and consistent financial operations but also from national bond rating agencies which hold our local governments in high esteem. In 1994, for example, more than 25 percent of all Triple-A rated local government units in the nation were in North Carolina. Significant also is the important fact that there has not been a bond payment default in North Carolina by any general purpose government entity since the Great Depression.

To be sure, this fine record of fiscal responsibility is a source of pride for all North Carolinians. But it is more than that. It is also a source of considerable savings. In a typical year, the Treasurer's Office will sell more than $1 billion worth of bonds for local governments. These bonds are sold at interest rates considerably below the national Bond-Buyer's Index, because of our Triple-A credit rating, which results in considerable savings for North Carolina taxpayers.

In 1993, the bonded indebtedness by local county, city and special tax districts totaled $5.1 billion. In addition, there was an additional outstanding $11.5 billion in revenue and special obligation bonds. Together with the State's $581 million in outstanding bonds this represented a total indebtedness by the State and its subdivisions of more than $18 billion. However, in view of the State's $99 billion annual gross product, this was a modest level of debt and well within the ability of the citizens to pay.

Summary

While the basic organization of local government has not changed much since early Colonial years, the scope and the relationship between State and local government has changed immensely. North Carolina's centralized method of raising revenue at the state level and using the 100 counties as principal agents for delivering essential services has resulted in a fair and equitable system for all of the State's citizens.

Today, local governments in North Carolina levy and collect only about 28 percent of the total revenue used to finance State and local services. Yet, they make 57 percent of all direct general expenditures and employ 70 percent of all State and local government workers.

While this unique partnership between State and local governments has been taken for granted in our State, most other states have yet to take advantage of this simple, yet both practical and efficient method of funding and administering public services.

This system of "shared responsibility" was an invention of necessity in 1931, when the Governor and members of the General Assembly wrestled with the most devastating economic crises ever to confront North Carolina. Their solution has resulted in a sound partnership between the State and local governments that has become the envy of other local government officials throughout the nation.

Chapter 9

Managing The Public's Money

Our frugal heritage; our system of checks and balances; and our prudent policies have contributed to a well-managed system of public finance in North Carolina. But, there is growing evidence we must do a much better job in the future.

Our governments are in deep trouble today... We last reinvented our governments during the early decades of the 20th Century, roughly from 1900 through 1940... Today, the world of government is once again in great flux. The emergence of a postindustrial knowledge-based, global economy has undermined old realities throughout the world, creating wonderful opportunities and frightening problems.

David Osborne and Ted Gaebler, *Reinventing Government: How the Entrepreneurial Spirit is Transforming the Public Sector*

We have done a good job of managing public finance in North Carolina. Our well-defined system of checks and balances, our strong sense of frugality handed down generation by generation from a long line of fiscally conservative leaders, and the high expectations of our citizens are significant factors in why this is so.

Our fiscal affairs have been in order for so long that this practice has given birth to the popular saying, "In North Carolina, good government is a habit," and justifiably so. The best evidence of our financial prudence is a consistently balanced budget, which probably would be balanced in North Carolina even if the State Constitution did not require it. The State's business leaders during the past half century would not tolerate the kind of irresponsibility that has lead to havoc in other states, or the crushing national debt, which now threatens the economic stability of this country.

The concept of public finance management has grown in recent years to include not only the necessity of accounting for public monies to make sure they are spent as authorized, and also to include the requirement that the public need for various expenditures be revisited and re-examined. In discharging our duty to the public to safeguard public resources, it is no longer sufficient to audit expenditures after they've been made, but it has become necessary to question proposed expenditures to determine if they are within the scope of our constitutional mandate for "a public purpose."

For many years in our State's history, the cost of the General Assembly–member salaries and their travel and subsistence for biennial sessions–was the largest single State expenditure. In fact, until just a century ago the amount of funds which the General Assembly appropriated for its own operation exceeded all of the other State expenditures. In fiscal 1994, the $25 million budget of the General Assembly was only a drop in the State's nearly $16.7 billion budget.

Government expenditures have grown rapidly in recent years, resulting in a larger and far more complex bureaucracy. The need for better management of our public sector has become a major concern. No longer is it sufficient to know that public monies are being spent for the purposes for which they were authorized. It has become important that we re-examine the need for government programs, to re-assure ourselves they are still worthwhile and that they serve a valid public purpose.

North Carolina's State budget increased 138 percent during the 1980s and in doing so, our State earned the dubious honor of experiencing the eighth fastest growth of any state budget in the country. Revenues increased 137 percent during the same period while the state-funded workforce grew by 41 percent.

As an example of the meteoric growth which North Carolina has seen recently, it took us 200 years to reach our first $4 billion budget in 1978; yet, this doubled in just the next eight years, by 1986. The North Carolina budget doubled again in eight years in 1994. In just 16 years, from 1978 to 1994, State spending quadrupled. There is little evidence to suggest that the quality of public services improved in equal measure during that period of time, leaving us with a growing demand for closer scrutiny of how we manage and spend public funds.

North Carolina's Constitution includes three important provisions regarding the management of our public funds. First, it requires a balanced operating budget. In Article III, Section Four, Paragraph Three, the Governor is charged with preparing and recommending to the General Assembly a balanced budget each biennium. The North Carolina Constitution specifically states in this section, "The total expenditures of the State for the fiscal period covered by the budget shall not exceed the total of receipts during that fiscal period and the surplus remaining in the State Treasury at the beginning of the period."

Second, the Constitution stipulates that tax funds be used "for the public purpose only."

And third, the Constitution strictly limits the manner and extent by which public debt can be created both by State and local governments. Local governments generally can incur debt (general obligation bonds) only by the vote of a majority of its citizens and even then the manner in which local governments incur debt is done under the watchful eye and approval of the Local Government Commission. (See Chapter Eight for a more complete discussion of local government finance.) At the State level, the Constitution also requires a majority vote of the qualified voters of the State before incurring debt that is backed by the full faith and credit of the State.

There is no doubt that this constitutional restraint in levying taxes, spending public funds, and creating debt has contributed significantly to sound financial policies. The organization of our State government is also an important factor.

Checks and Balances

North Carolina's strong Council of State system, where not only the Governor is elected statewide, but also nine cabinet offices are popularly elected, creates an important system of checks and balances that has served in the best interest of the State's citizens. In North Carolina the following officials are popularly elected: Lieutenant Governor, Secretary of State, Auditor, Treasurer, Superintendent of Public Instruction, Attorney General, Commissioner of Agriculture, Commissioner of Labor, and Commissioner of Insurance. Along with the Governor, their elections are held every four years during general elections simultaneous with balloting for the President of the United States.

The popular election of these officials offers voters much greater control by the people over each of the offices than if their department heads were appointed by the Governor and/or legislature and subject to removal. In the Treasurer's Office, for example, voters may hold the Treasurer directly accountable for the manner in which public funds are managed and invested. There is clear evidence that voters have reacted strongly when they learned that State funds were left "idle" and did not earn as much interest as they could have with more prudent management. This happened in the election of 1948, when Treasurer Charles Johnson ran for Governor as the favorite of most Democratic party leaders. He had served ably as Treasurer for 15 years and was credited with offering strong leadership in the office during the difficult years in which the State was recovering from the Great Depression. However, during the campaign of 1948, one of the issues raised against Treasurer Johnson was the fact that State funds under his control and supervision had not been invested properly, resulting in the loss of potential interest earnings for taxpayers. This was a significant issue in Johnson's loss to W. Kerr Scott, who won the Democratic primary election and went on to become the "Good Roads Governor" and later, United States Senator.

Three elected State officers play separate but important roles in safeguarding North Carolina public funds. The Governor, as Director of the Budget and Chief Executive Officer of the State, is involved in both budgeting and administering public funds. The Treasurer, as custodian of all public funds, is charged with making sure that enough money is on hand at all times to meet the State's needs. Also, the Treasurer has the responsibility of making sure that funds are spent for the purpose for which they were authorized by the General Assembly. If the Treasurer has reason to believe that funds are about to be spent for an unlawful or unauthorized purpose, he must act to prevent that from happening. The State Auditor, who is also elected statewide, is charged with the task of monitoring and accounting for public expenditures. The Auditor systematically reviews State agencies to make sure that all funds are both accounted for and are spent specifically for the purposes as authorized by the General Assembly.

When the Auditor finds the misuse, mis-management, waste, or other instances of inappropriate use of public funds, he is required to take appropriate action. In extreme cases, law enforcement authorities are brought in when larceny, embezzlement and other crimes are suspected. There have been dramatic cases of abuse by a few State employees. In the 1950s a popular Raleigh developer was convicted of influence-peddling in the sale of paint to the Department of Transportation. He was convicted and sentenced to prison, as was the owner of an advertising agency in the mid-1970s who was found falsifying invoices in connection with the tourism advertising program. In the early 1990s, the purchase of several million dollars of excess clothing was revealed in the Department of Correction. These and other discrepancies in the use of public funds were discovered by the system of checks and balances that has served North Carolina well. In many cases, when the Auditor finds relative minor discrepancies, sufficient corrective action is taken by the executive branch.

While not perfect, government in North Carolina has been exceptionally clean and scandal-free. That is due in large part to the fact that our officeholders know they have to face the voters every four years and, therefore, must be diligent in the management of their affairs. Major credit is also due the citizens of this State for electing trustworthy leaders.

Faith and Trust of the People

In a democracy, the ultimate measure of success of government lies in the esteem with which it is held by the people served. The people who pay taxes and vote for officeholders have the power in each election to change the direction of their government by their choices at the ballot box.

We have seen enormous swings in public opinion at the national level in recent years and many of these came in direct response to strong public perceptions. President Lyndon Johnson was elected by a landslide in 1964, but four years later found himself so out of favor with voters that he dared not run for re-election. President Richard Nixon, too, was highly popular in his huge margin of victory in 1972, only to find himself the target of such a strong impeachment initiative that he became the first American President to resign in office, before his second term was half complete. President George Bush saw his 90 percent favorable poll ratings, resulting from his handling of the Gulf War, drop precipitously as voters turned their attention to a faltering economy. In 1992, President Bush became the second American President seeking re-election to be defeated in the last quarter of this century. His defeat was due almost altogether to the fact that voters disapproved of the way he managed the economy. Only one President, Ronald Reagan, has served two complete terms since 1960.

These voting trends say much about the changing mood of our citizens and they send a strong signal to officeholders that the voter is becoming more sophisticated and more demanding in the exercise of public power.

In North Carolina, we have experienced a similar upheaval. The State was governed for the first three-quarters of this century by the Democratic Party, though this was not necessarily a strictly one-party affair. While the Democratic Party won all elections for Governor between 1900 and 1972, there existed a loose two-party system within the ranks of the Democratic Party, where progressive and conservative factions competed for control.

Progressive elements prevailed in the late 1940s under Governor W. Kerr Scott who led a massive roadbuilding program, and again in the early 1960s, under Governor Terry Sanford, who pushed a renewed effort to improve education. Alternately the progressives were supplanted by conservatives who governed with a more laid-back style of leadership that enabled voters and taxpayers to catch their breath.

It was the defection in 1972 of a large segment of the conservative wing of the North Carolina Democratic Party, after the progressives captured the primary nomination for Governor, that resulted in the election of the first Republican Governor in this century. That election and the subsequent election of another Republican Governor in 1984, foreshadowed a major shift in policy making, including fiscal policy, in North Carolina.

During the 1980s, the Democrat-controlled General Assembly developed a tighter hold on the State's purse strings, particularly in dealing with the various agencies under the control of the Republican Governor. It resulted in micro-management of various programs to the point where managers in State government complain they have little discretion in the operation of their programs.

Re-examining Government

I believe our government must change significantly. The change must come about in how we operate. To understand the change that must be made in the future, one only has to look at how much and how rapidly government has changed in the recent past.

Just a century ago, most of the tax revenues raised in North Carolina were levied on property and spent to make laws, protect the public safety, and operate a small but highly dedicated government workforce. In 1900, the State did not build nor maintain public roads. That duty was left to the counties. In 1900 the State did not incarcerate convicted criminals, except for the most incorrigible offenders who were kept at Central Prison in Raleigh. Other criminals were kept in county jails, maintained by the counties, where the high sheriff hanged those condemned to die.

In 1900, the State did not consider education a major public responsibility even though the Constitution of 1868 had included the right to an education as a basic right of each citizen.

Except for providing the barest form of relief to only those in the starkest of circumstances—the criminally insane, the crippled, the lame—the State did not offer much in the way of public welfare.

Today, of course, everything is different. The State, in cooperation with the federal government, provides all of the funding to build and maintain North Carolina's 77,000 miles of public roads, the largest State-maintained highway system in America. There are few complaints about highway expenditures because our citizens see the results of that program every day. Our good roads are a major asset in attracting new jobs and building a strong infrastructure.

The State provides two-thirds of the funding for public schools. The State now operates most of the public safety and justice systems. And, the State has assumed a major responsibility for providing income for the poor, health care for the indigent, temporary income for the unemployed, and, long-term care for the infirm and aged.

The State, in its desire to provide for not only the safety but also the health and welfare of its citizens, has come around to the notion that it should also provide for their cultural aggrandizement as well. In its aim to uplift the spiritual and aesthetic quality of its citizens, it has chosen to establish one of the most elegant public art museums in the nation. The North Carolina Symphony fills the ears of little children and adults throughout the State with the most beautiful symphonic music many of them will ever hear. In Winston-Salem, North Carolina taxpayers operate a unique School of the Arts for its native sons and daughters, as well as students from all across the nation.

This government subsidy of the arts has led to a contentious national debate because of the controversial nature of some of the projects funded. While proponents of this government funding defend the use of public monies as a right protected by the First Amendment, they cannot find a constitutional basis for requiring taxpayers to fund such expenditures, which benefit only a few people.

A few decades ago, the North Carolina General Assembly heard the pleas from a group of citizens seeking an initial appropriation for a State zoo. The legislature was promised by eager zoo enthusiasts that they would never ask for more State funds because donations from private sponsors and income from visitors would be adequate for all future needs. The leader of zoo supporters, himself a prominent citizen with great credibility, assured members of the General Assembly that they would never again hear another request from the zoo for State funding. Zoo supporters did come back in desperation a few years later, and now the operation of the North Carolina Zoo at Asheboro is a significant part of the annual budget of the Department of Environment, Health, and Natural Resources. At the same time the State agreed to assume the burden of operating this excellent State zoo, it was allowing its State Parks system to deteriorate into arguably the worst state park system in the nation.

Through its generous arts grants, the State subsidizes the writing of poetry and fiction, painting, and numerous other artistic endeavors which could not otherwise be sustained.

In the interest of creating jobs for its people, the State has done much to help private industry make money. It underwrites research, builds water and sewer lines, constructs roads, and provides expertise in marketing, export, and other areas of primary interest to a limited circle of entrepreneurs.

We do not mean to suggest that any of these State-funded programs are illegal. They are all noble gestures from a benevolent citizenry. But are they in the true definition expenditures for a purely public purpose? And, were these decisions made in a thoughtful, prudent manner that allowed our policy makers to understand the full range of consequences of their decisions? For example, it is doubtful that our leaders in the General Assembly would have been so eager to create the State Zoo if they had realized that the State parks system would become so strapped for operating funds that the snack bar at Mount Mitchell State Park would be forced to close for a summer in the mid-1980s, due to raw sewage leaking into the only well at North Carolina's highest summit; there was no money for repairs.

Education

No one now questions the duty of the State to take the lead in educating its people, particularly the children who are our future. Without an educated workforce our economy cannot compete in the modern, high tech, global economy. Without an educated citizenry our representative democracy will not survive.

Our State has made a tremendous commitment to education in this century, beginning in 1900 with the election of Charles Aycock as Governor, the first modern champion of a free public education for all of the State's children. It was just after 1900, with 400,000 school-age children enrolled, that annual public school spending in North Carolina first reached $1 million. Our schools were ranked last among the 48 states at that time.

In fiscal 1994, school enrollment was 1.1 million and total public school spending had increased to more than $5 billion. We were tied for 48th in the SAT scores of our children. The failure of our schools is manifest in far greater terms than poor test scores. Teenage pregnancies, escalating juvenile crime rates, and the growing public assistance rolls are far greater symptoms of a failing public school system.

These indicators seem to say we have not done a very good job managing the public funds entrusted to North Carolina's public schools in the 20th century. Since 1900, student enrollment increased two and one-half times and spending increased 5,000 times. And at the end of this cycle of escalating public spending, our schools were still among the very worst in the nation. While the taxpayer has been asked time and time again to pay more for schools, there have been few resultant improvements in the outcome.

What should have happened? First, instead of accepting the tired argument that more money is the solution to all education problems, the General Assembly should have scrutinized the programs it was funding. For example, the number of non-instructional education employees has increased to the point where teachers account for less than one-half of the total 131,000 school employees. At a time when most agree our student-teacher ratio is too high, this does not make sense.

Second, expectations have been lowered both for teachers and students and our schools are failing to achieve even minimally acceptable academic goals.

Third, we have allowed our public schools to become a battleground for social change instead of a place for learning. This has led to a breakdown in discipline, increased violence, and a growing number of intrusions and interruptions in what should normally be a quiet, serene place for learning.

These changes have taken place neither because our schools are inherently bad nor because the people who run them are bad managers. Our schools have failed to measure up to our expectations because we have allowed this to happen.

To address each of the concerns, we should have done some of the following. First, as we increased school spending, we should have included specific tangible measures of accountability that would have allowed parents and taxpayers to know in easy-to-understand laymen terms just how well their neighborhood schools were performing. The next step is obvious. In those specific schools where students were failing to achieve satisfactory progress, drastic changes in policy and personnel should have been made.

Second, higher standards should have been set long ago for teachers whose superior performance is critical to learning. You can no more have good schools without competent teachers than you can expect to fly safely in an airplane without a competent pilot.

Unless we recapture our public schools and demand a civilized code of conduct, our schools of the 21st century will look like prisons and will have to be built like security chambers, rather than high tech laboratories. There are a number of effective tools for encouraging good behavior. Tying the driving privileges of young people to conduct and success in school will get their attention quickly. Assigning disruptive students to alternative schools, set up to handle students with behavior problems will separate the troublemakers but continue to give them an opportunity to learn. And finally, we ought to hold parents more accountable for the conduct of their children until children have received at least a high school diploma.

These are elementary things which could be done quickly at a nominal cost to improve our schools. But it will take courage to implement these changes. It is imperative that we take charge of our public schools and require them to do the job they are supposed to do in educating our children. The future of our State and our country depends upon it. Our future in this democracy depends on an educated and civilized citizenry. To fail this important task means certain anarchy.

Justice System

Our justice system is also in great need of repair. The courts are congested. Our prisons are full and have become a revolving door for dangerous criminals, who, even when convicted for heinous crimes, are detained for only a small portion of their sentence and are released back to inflict more harm on society.

In 1993, it was revealed that the State spends $10 million more each year to defend indigent defendants than it spends to prosecute all criminals. The knowledge that we spend nearly a quarter billion dollars a year to operate the courts and district attorney offices, and another $500 million to house some 21,000 prison inmates is not reassuring. Neither is it comforting to know that, for the same amount which it costs taxpayers to keep a criminal in prison, four students could attend the University of North Carolina for an entire year.

There is a compelling argument that our increased prison costs are directly related to our low-performing education system. In view of the fact that 90 percent of the prison inmates are high school dropouts without job skills, it follows then that if we could reduce the number of dropouts, we probably would reduce the number of prison inmates.

The solution to this dilemma is not an easy one, as members of the General Assembly found out when they gathered in Raleigh during February of 1994. They met in a special session, called by Governor Jim Hunt, to address the crisis of crime which existed at that time. During that special session, the General Assembly appropriated nearly $300 million for programs designed to reduce crime.

Welfare

In fiscal 1994, the $5.3 billion budget of the Department of Human Resources, half of it from federal funds, was the second largest item in the State budget. Only education receives more public funds. Welfare and health care for the indigent is also the fastest growing part of the State budget.

The initial philosophy of public welfare grew from the concept that government ought to provide a safety net to help those who are truly needy–the handicapped, mentally ill and others, who because of physical or mental limitations, cannot take care of themselves. That concept has been vastly expanded today to include many who can take care of themselves but because of their impoverished circumstances and often because of their own choices, have become wards of the State. We are rewarding failure, seemingly content to do so indefinitely.

The North Carolina Department of Human Resources employs 17,000 workers who provide a variety of services to nearly a million constituents. There is a growing perception among taxpayers that this is one area of public spending in need of better management or else it will continue to grow until public assistance is the largest single item in the budget.

GPAC: An Opportunity Lost

In 1991, the North Carolina General Assembly appropriated $3 million for a comprehensive study of State government operations. A nationally acclaimed consultant was hired to conduct a two-year long study, examine all State government programs, identify waste, duplication, and inefficiency, and report back to the 1993 session with specific recommendations for ways to save money. This initiative was called the Government Performance Audit Commission (GPAC).

Out of hundreds of recommendations which GPAC said would reduce government spending by $275 million annually, the 1993 General Assembly adopted only five recommendations accounting for some $30 million in savings during the 1993-94 fiscal year, and $43 million the following year.

What the General Assembly did was a far cry from what many of its members said they would do during their 1992 campaigns for re-election. GPAC was a big issue in all of the close races. Incumbents pointed to potential big savings in making State government operations more efficient, as an alternative to raising taxes. But when they got down to the unpleasant task of reducing or eliminating specific programs, the General Assembly could not reach a consensus. Although GPAC identified a number of programs in drastic need of change, when it came time to make tough decisions, legislators couldn't say no to defenders of the status quo.

Reinventing Government

In their book, *Reinventing Government: How the Entrepreneurial Spirit is Transforming the Public Sector,* David Osborne and Ted Gaebler discuss the crisis that has developed in American government as it moves into its third century. They suggest that nothing less than a major transformation in the way that government seeks to achieve its noble goals will allow this republic to survive.

To improve our schools, which get nearly two-thirds of all the tax funds raised in North Carolina, we should require their leaders to do the job which they were hired to do, or replace them with others.

To improve our justice and public safety system, we should expand the prison system so that decent, law-abiding citizens can be safe from those who are prone to rob, rape, murder and steal. A surplus capacity in the penal system is a strong deterrent to crime. But we should also make sure that our education system is discharging its duty to those in greatest need of help staying out of trouble with the law.

There is no question that we have become too generous with public money. Taxpayers resent it. Those who benefit from government largess don't appreciate it, but do expect more.

In the twilight years of all great civilizations–the Greeks, the Romans, and the British–the heavy burden of domestic spending resulted in higher and higher taxes. When the taxes reached levels that constituents considered oppressive, they resisted and the empires crumbled from within. In each of these great civilizations, which in their days were the most powerful military rulers of the world, it was the loss of faith among their own people, not the might of outside threats, that brought these once great empires to their knees.

There are similar twists and turns in the story of our own nation. Our forefathers first came to this continent to avoid oppressive taxes and intrusive government policies which interfered with their strong religious convictions. Remember the Boston Tea Party and the ensuing debate in Philadelphia over "taxation without representation?" Modern day tax protestors do not throw tea into the sea. They organize to defeat incumbent politicians who spend public funds unwisely.

The fact that a proposed balanced budget amendment to our nation's constitution came within a half dozen votes of getting the necessary two-thirds majority in the House of Representatives in 1992 indicates the widespread concern for this issue.

We are close again to the precipice that inspired the poetic words of Thomas Jefferson in the opening paragraph of the Declaration of Independence, "When in the course of human events, it becomes necessary..."

It has become necessary, in my opinion, for a drastic new look at government, at the federal level, and especially at the State level, to redefine what we want from our public servants and to restructure government so that once again government serves the people, not vice versa.

Chapter 10

The State Treasurer, Keeper of the Public Purse

North Carolina's State Treasurer has more constitutional and statutory duties than any other elected public official in the State except for the Governor.

As the State's banker and chief financial officer, the Treasurer plays a crucial role in the operation of State government because, in one way or another, money is required to pay for every single government program, act and deed. To a large degree, the financial reputation of the State among the national and world financial markets is determined by the Treasurer, who is also judged on the basis of his personal integrity, experience and judgment.

The Treasurer's most important duty is to serve as the State's banker, managing and investing all public North Carolina funds. With a budget of $16.7 billion in fiscal 1994, daily deposits often exceeding $100 million, and with financial assets totaling more than $30 billion, that is a formidable job. The work of the Department of the Treasurer touches the life of every citizen of North Carolina in many different ways.

It is the duty of the Treasurer to make sure there is enough money on hand at all times to pay the State's bills in a timely manner and to invest temporarily idle funds until they are needed. In 1993, for example, these investments earned $2.2 billion and provided a net return of 8.49 percent.

One of the best indications of the financial health of a State, or a business, is its credit rating. North Carolina's Triple-A credit rating, the highest rating given, is now taken for granted. However, it was a long time coming and it was not easy to achieve. Not until 1960, almost 30 years after the Great Depression, and well after the General Assembly had demonstrated its commitment to sound fiscal management and a balanced budget, did North Carolina receive its Triple-A credit rating.

A state's credit rating is determined by three major national rating agencies–Standard and Poor's, Moody's and Fitch's–and is based upon the amount of investment or credit risk believed to exist in the State's ability to repay its bonded indebtedness. The higher the rating, the lower

Table 10-1. North Carolina Treasurer's Investment Earnings, 1942-1994

	General Fund	Highway Funds	Pension Trust Funds	Other Funds	Total All Funds
1942-51	5,103,900		8,194,000		13,297,900
1952-61	36,612,078		68,468,000		105,080,078
1962-71	138,079,098	67,721,332	319,161,000		524,961,430
1972-81	566,517,029	158,283,321	2,047,609,149	40,104,470	2,812,513,969
1982-91	1,219,967,995	306,605,240	10,527,786,785	767,543,556	12,821,903,576
1992	56,898,765	42,659,680	1,694,271,198	135,468,030	1,929,297,673
1993	77,910,893	42,826,103	1,904,054,068	147,295,214	2,172,086,278
1994	122,828,342	40,612,781	*1,994,378,565	113,579,837	*2,271,399,525
Total	2,223,918,100	658,708,457	18,563,922,765	1,203,991,107	22,650,540,429

Source: North Carolina Treasurer's Report, 1994
*1994 Pension Trust Funds and Total All Funds, includes earnings through March 31, 1994

the risk of an investment. A Triple-A credit rating is not only prestigious but also means important savings for taxpayers, since bonds sold with this rating result in lower interest costs.

Criteria used to establish this rating include the State's fiscal history, current financial performance and economic data. Other factors include the State's outstanding debt, the ability to repay its debt, and its taxing power and resources behind the debt. The fact that neither the State of North Carolina nor any of its local government entities have defaulted on any public debt since the Great Depression is an important consideration, as is the fact that the State's Constitution requires a balanced budget each year.

Much importance is given to the attitude and character of the State's people and the way they hold officeholders accountable. Leadership, particularly the State's financial leadership, is also important. Responsible leadership in the Treasurer's Office is vital. We have been fortunate in North Carolina to have had the service of many strong-willed Treasurers, whose prudent financial leadership prevailed in times of crisis. Their leadership, time and time again, has kept North Carolina from adopting financial policies which have resulted in problems in other states.

While quality credit ratings are difficult to establish they are easy to lose. During periods of economic downturns, government revenues often decline as spending demands continue to increase, thus placing great pressure upon elected officials to maintain an adequate level of public services and a balanced budget. North Carolina's Triple-A credit rating was threatened briefly in 1991, as the State faced a potential $1.3 billion budget shortfall, caused by a recessionary decline in revenue well below what the Governor and General Assembly had projected. Rating agencies watched North Carolina leaders closely as they dealt with this problem, which was solved by more than $600 million in higher taxes and an equal amount of reduction in proposed government spending. These two dramatic actions helped balance the State's budget and did much to preserve its financial reputation.

In 1994, North Carolina was one of only four states that maintained its Triple-A rating by all three rating agencies. At that same time, nine units of local government within the State also had a Triple-A rating. They were: Charlotte, Mecklenburg County, Durham, Durham County, Greensboro, Raleigh, Wake County, Winston-Salem, and the Durham and Wake County Special Airport District. In fact, at that time, 25 percent of all Triple-A rated units of state and local government nationwide were in North Carolina, according to Standard and Poor's ratings.

Organization of the Treasurer's Office

The Treasurer's Office is organized into four divisions. Each division is responsible for a specific duty vitally important to the operation and management of North Carolina's fiscal affairs. The Investment and Banking Division handles the day-to-day banking duties and invests the State's several trust funds and surplus operational funds. The State and Local Government Finance Division provides local governments throughout North Carolina with staff assistance in discharging their financial and record-keeping responsibilities. The Retirement Systems Division administers the retirement benefit plans for North Carolina's more than 500,000 active and retired public employees.

The Administrative Services Division provides support services to the Treasurer and other divisions within the Office of the Treasurer, while also administering the State's Escheat and Unclaimed Property Program.

The Investment and Banking Division

The primary duty of the State Treasurer is to manage the cash flow of the State's annual budget and to manage the financial assets of the various trust funds. It is the Treasurer's singular responsibility to take custody of these funds and manage them in the best interest of the public. This duty is discharged through the Investment and Banking Division.

Banking Operations. The Treasurer operates a highly sophisticated and centralized system for receiving and disbursing State funds, as provided for by the General Assembly. Rather than each of the hundreds of State agencies having its own separate bank account, each agency maintains an account with the State Treasurer, who provides the same service that a commercial bank would normally offer.

This system provides for quick and efficient concentration of State assets and allows immediate investment of temporarily idle funds, so that the State and its citizens receive the full benefits of all public resources.

Cash Management. All revenues collected by a State agency are deposited daily with the Treasurer for credit to the entity's budget code account. For most entities located in Raleigh, deposits are made directly with the Investment and Banking Division's "teller window" in the Albemarle Building. The Division processes these deposits and prepares "cash letters" to be presented to corresponding depository banks for collection. For agencies located outside Raleigh, the Division has arranged for banks and savings institutions to accept deposits, which are consolidated immediately into the Treasurer's central account in Raleigh. Daily cash deposits by State agencies located throughout North Carolina vary from $60 million on a "slow" day to as much as $100 million or more on busier days. State agencies make more than 250,000 deposits at some 700 different depositories each year.

North Carolina uses a warrant system to disburse funds. Whenever a State agency proposes or acts to disburse funds, it issues warrants (checks) against a disbursing account maintained with the Treasurer. The warrants bear the North Carolina Treasurer's own American Banking Association (ABA) transit routing number and are payable at par through the Federal Reserve System. North Carolina was the first State to be assigned its own ABA transit routing number by the Federal Reserve System. The warrants are deposited by recipients into the commercial banking system and are ultimately presented to the Treasurer for payment.

Daily warrant clearings are accepted from the Federal Reserve Bank, the State Employees' Credit Union, and nine correspondent commercial banks desiring to present warrants directly to the State Treasurer, as opposed to "clearing" these items through the Federal Reserve System. The Treasurer processes more than 21 million warrants annually. The main advantage of the warrant system is that the banker's "float," and the earnings thereon are retained by the State.

Investment Management. On a daily basis the Treasurer tracks the cash flow of the General and Highway Funds, as well as the cash balances of the trust funds under management and computes the amount available for investment. Any surplus is invested in various short-term instruments as authorized by State law and in accordance with projected cash flow needs. Among the more popular short-term options are certificates of deposit and saving certificates issued by North Carolina banks and savings institutions. The Treasurer sets the interest rate, which by State law must be the same as current market rates available for U.S. Government and/or Agency securities. Certificates are purchased for a term of six months and scheduled to mature weekly to assure a steady cash flow.

Earnings from the Treasurer's investments (often for overnight or for a weekend) contribute substantially to the financial resources of the State. To illustrate the impact of daily deposits and prompt concentration of the State's financial assets, a calculation was made recently of the interest earned as the result of strict adherence to this policy. It totaled approximately $41,000 per day or $15 million in a single year. This is a sufficient amount of money to operate the Department of the State Treasurer for an entire year. So, just by making sure the Treasurer receives the daily deposits promptly and invests them prudently, the Department of the Treasurer earns its keep. As of June 30, 1994, State funds under the Treasurer's management totaled $30 billion. These included assets of the four separate pension systems, miscellaneous trust funds and the General and Highway Funds.

Earnings on all State funds in 1993 totaled $2.2 billion for a net return of 8.49 percent. Investment earnings on the retirement funds in that same year exceeded the combined employer and employee contributions, a significant achievement for both State employees and taxpayers.

Trust Funds Investment. The Trust Funds are composed primarily of the holdings of the four retirement systems, the two largest being the Teachers' and State Employees' Retirement System and the Local Governmental Employees' Retirement System. Of all the Trust Fund assets under management, 98 percent belong to these retirement systems.

The assets of these retirement systems are among the State's most important and most carefully managed resources. North Carolina is unique in that the investment integrity is dictated by the State Constitution which prohibits any use of these funds for any purpose except for retirement benefits. Article V, Section 6, paragraph 2 of the North Carolina Constitution is quite specific and restrictive in how these retirement funds may

Table 10-2. Treasurer's Investment Pool by Type and Segment (as of June 30, 1994)

Security Type	Short-term Portfolio	Long-term Portfolio	Equity Portfolio	Total All Portfolios
Repurchase Agreements	372,030,000			372,030,000
Certificates of Deposit	111,546,000			111,546,000
Treasury & Agency Securities	5,545,308,239	6,386,605,738		11,931,913,977
Corporate Bonds	10,000,000	6,633,469,695		6,643,469,695
International Bonds		467,246,059		
Mortgage Backed Securities (GNMA's)		3,235,688,093		3,235,688,093
Long-term COD's		10,000,000		10,000,000
Equity Securities				
Common Stock			5,719,426,517	5,719,426,517
Trust Funds			1,487,684,210	1,487,684,210
Mutual Funds			5,405,780	5,405,780
Real Estate Investments			243,913,623	243,913,623
Venture Capital			28,842,911	
Total Investments (Book)	$6,038,884,239	$16,733,009,585	7,485,273,041	$30,257,166,865
Percent of Total Book Value	19.96%	55.30%	24.74%	100.00%
Total Investments (Market)	$6,017,999,415	$17,241,060,881	9,313,739,573	$30,572,799,869
Percent of Total Market Value	18.48%	52.93%	28.59%	100.00%

Source: North Carolina Treasurer's Report, 1994
Book and Market Values for Venture Capital and Real Estate are as of March 31, 1994

be used. It reads: "Neither the General Assembly nor any public officer, employee or agency shall use or authorize to be used any part of the funds of the Teachers' and State Employees' Retirement System or the Local Governmental Employees Retirement System for any purpose other than retirement system benefits and purposes, administrative expenses, and refunds; except that retirement system funds may be invested as authorized by law, subject to the investment limitation that the funds of the Teacher's and State Employees' Retirement System and the Local Governmental Employees' Retirement System shall not be applied, diverted or loaned to, or used by the State, any State agency, State officer, public officer, or public employee."

Investment Pools. Investment objectives of both the cash management and the trust funds investment programs are achieved through participation in one or more co-mingled portfolios, called funds or investment pools, established by the Treasurer as authorized by State law.

The objective for all investment programs is to generate maximum income consistent with safety of principal. Liquidity is also important, since the Treasurer's cash balances are ultimately subject to disbursement upon presentation of valid warrants.

There are strict requirements for choosing investments prescribed by law, such as the stipulation that only investment grade stocks, bonds, and securities can be purchased. This requirement justifiably limits consideration to securities in investor-owned companies with a credit rating of grade A or better. In practice, however, securities are seldom purchased with a credit rating lower than Double-A (Aa).

Investment strategies focus on such things as quality of credit, maturity, market fluctuation, interest rate trends, and projections. The strategies differ with each of the funds. Safety of principal and liquidity generally take precedence over yield; however, in some cases, yield potential may outweigh liquidity.

Maturities in the Short-Term Investment Fund range from overnight to seven years and account for about 15 percent of the State's total financial assets. They include monies from the General and Highway Funds and temporary funds belonging to all other participating entities which are not otherwise invested in other portfolios.

The objective of the Long-Term Investment Fund, begun in 1941, is to provide the maximum, long-term, high-yield, safe return on the fixed-income investments of the North Carolina retirement systems, and other participants required or permitted to deposit funds with the State Treasurer. This fund represents the largest concentration of assets and accounts for 60 percent of the State's total investment assets. Fixed income securities such as U.S. Treasury and Agency securities, investment grade corporate bonds, international securities, and long-term certificates of deposits are used to achieve the goals of this fund.

Equity Investments. In 1961, the Equity Investment Fund was established exclusively for the State-administered retirement systems to generate long-term appreciation, while providing a hedge during periods of moderate inflation. The goal of this fund, which accounts for approximately 25 percent of the State's total investment assets, is to generate a return exceeding that of the Standard and Poor's composite Stock Index (S&P 500), on a trailing 36-month basis. Currently there are seven distinct and actively managed investment pools within the Equity Investment Fund.

The Real Estate Investment Fund, established in 1984, provides a vehicle for long-term growth of capital through investment in shares of beneficial interests in real estate. Positive real rates of return and additional diversification are goals of this fund which consists of only about one percent of the State's total investment assets.

The Venture Capital Investment Fund was established in 1988, as a vehicle to provide potentially high asset growth and encourage the creation of new jobs in business and industry. The fund's strategy is to establish and maintain a broadly diversified venture capital portfolio. As is the nature of venture capital, returns are expected to be low in the early years, but there is a reasonable expectation of significant gains in later years as the entrepreneurs funded by this capital succeed. Initial investments of this venture capital were limited to $20 million; however, in 1990 the General Assembly authorized venture capital investments or corporate buyout transactions of up to $30 million. In recognition of the volatile nature of venture capital investments, only a small portion of the State's assets are allocated to this fund, which in 1994 accounted for a mere 0.10 percent of the State's total assets.

The objective of the Bond Proceeds Fund, which consists of separate portfolios for the general obligation bonds sold by the State since 1986, is to provide maximum income within the bounds of the IRS regulations on bond transactions.

In the Liquid Asset Fund, liquidity is a prime concern since these funds are subject to immediate withdrawal without notice. Securities are marked to market to reflect current prices daily and earnings are automatically reinvested. This fund generally accounts for less than four percent of the State's total investment assets.

The State and Local Government Finance Division

The State and Local Government Finance Division provides local governments throughout North Carolina with staff assistance in fiscal administration and in debt management. This duty is discharged primarily through the Local Government Commission, an agency created during the Great Depression at the request of local government leaders.

The Local Government Commission. Through the Local Government Commission, expertise is made available to local governments in managing their bonded indebtedness and in managing current fiscal operations. This service of the Treasurer's Office has become a great asset for local government officials throughout the State and has resulted in lower bond interest costs and millions of dollars in savings to taxpayers.

The Local Government Commission is a uniquely important agency in North Carolina. (See Chapter 8 for a more thorough discussion.) A unique feature of the Local Government Commission's power is its statutory authority to react quickly and decisively in the event of an imminent default in the timely payment of the debt obligations of the units of local government. Under certain circumstances, the Commission may remove public officials and levy local taxes to pay for public debt that has been incurred. While it has not been necessary to use this provision, the mere existence of this power has inspired respect by local officials and confidence by bond buyers.

As result of the leadership and prudence of the Local Government Commission, there has been no actual default of public debt by a general purpose local government unit in North Carolina since the Great Depression.

Debt Management. The Local Government Commission has final authority over whether and how local governments in North Carolina may incur debt. In reviewing a request for debt financing, usually through the sale of bonds, the Local Government Commission makes a thorough review of the financial and debt management practices of the unit, the size of the proposed issue, the effect upon the tax rate and the unit's compliance with the Local Government Budget and Fiscal Control Act. Only when the Commission is assured that the proposed debt is for a worthy and authorized public purpose and that the unit of local government is capable of making repayment does it give its blessing.

As of June 30, 1993, total indebtedness of the State of North Carolina and its local government entities exceeded $18.6 billion. This debt was allocated in the following manner: State $581 million; State authorities and institutions $9.5 billion; counties $3.0 billion; cities $2.7 billion; special districts and authorities $2.5 billion. In addition, there were $2.1 billion in bonds authorized but not yet issued.

Local governments benefit immensely by the State's Triple-A credit rating which results in lower interest rates that taxpayers pay on bonds. For example, in 1993, a total of $1.3 billion general obligation bonds were sold with interest rates averaging 84 basis points under the national Bond Buyer's Index. This resulted in a projected savings to North Carolina taxpayers of more than $102.9 million over the life of these bonds.

Fiscal Management. The Local Government Commission also has the responsibility to monitor current fiscal operations of local governments and to be alert for potential problems. As a result of this provision, the Division has been able, on numerous occasions, to identify small problems in local government finance and recommend corrective action before they became major problems.

The Commission has nine members: the Treasurer, who serves as Chairman; Secretary of State, State Auditor, Secretary of Revenue and five others by appointment (three by the Governor, one by the Lieutenant Governor, and one by the Speaker of the House of Representatives). The Treasurer selects the Secretary of the Commission who heads the administrative staff.

Assistance to Other Agencies. The State Treasurer provides assistance to other agencies whose statutory duties relate to the financial welfare of the State.

The North Carolina Solid Waste Management Capital Projects Financing Agency provides a loan fund for financing the capital expenses incurred in local and regional solid waste management programs. The Agency Board of Directors consists of five members: the Treasurer and four others by appointment (two by the Governor, one by the Speaker of the House of Representatives and one by the President Pro Tempore of the Senate).

Private institutions of higher education in North Carolina may receive financial assistance through bonds issued by the North Carolina Educational Facilities Finance Agency. Its Board of Directors is composed of seven members: the Treasurer, State Auditor and five others by appointment (three by the Governor, one by the Speaker of the House of Representatives and one by the President Pro Tempore of the Senate).

The Retirement Systems Division

The Retirement Systems Division administers the retirement benefit plans for the State's public employees. These include the Teachers' and State Employees' Retirement System, Local Governmental Employees' Retirement System, Firemen's and Rescue Workers' Pension Fund, Consolidated Judicial Retirement System and Legislative Retirement System. For the some 500,000 active and retired beneficiaries of the various public employee retirement systems, the work of this division is one of the Department's most important duties. During an average year, the Division will establish more than 37,000 new accounts and process benefits for more than 6,600 new retirees each year. Seventy percent of the State's retired public employees receive their monthly retirement checks, totaling some $80 million per month, through direct electronic deposit.

The purpose of a retirement system for public employees is to recruit and retain competent employees for a career in public service and provide a replacement income for retirement, disability, or, at death, for an employee's survivors.

Because of the wise planning and sound management of the public employees' pension funds, beneficiaries can look forward to a secure future during their retirement. As of December 31, 1992, the Teacher's and State Employee's Retirement System was 97 percent funded; Local Governmental Employees' Retirement System, 98 percent funded; and Consolidated Judicial Retirement System, 91 percent funded.

The ultimate vote of confidence was paid to the Treasurer's Office by beneficiaries of the State Retirement System in the few days after the precipitous 500-point fall of the stock market on that "Black Monday" in October of 1987. Amid great concern by investors everywhere for information about their holdings, we expected many calls and inquiries. However, the Treasurer's Office received only two telephone calls and one inquiry from a walk-in visitor who sought assurance that their State pension funds were secure. They were.

Administrative Services Division

The Administrative Services Division provides support services to the Treasurer and other divisions within the Department of the State Treasurer and administers the State's Escheat and Unclaimed Property Fund, which in 1993, had assets in excess of $109 million.

An escheat is the succession of abandoned property to the State. It is not a tax but results from the failure of a person legally entitled to the property to make a valid claim against the holder of the property within a prescribed period of time. The principle of escheat goes back to the days of the feudal landholding system in England, during the Middle Ages. It was based upon the premise that property, in the absence of a rightful owner or upon failure of any rightful heirs to take claim upon an owner's death, reverted to the Sovereign from whom all property rights derived.

In North Carolina, property is also escheated from the estate of a person dying intestate, without any known or discoverable heirs. Real or personal property which escheats under North Carolina law is liquidated and placed in the Escheat Fund, along with all other monies collected or earned. This property comes from banks and other financial institutions, insurance companies, hospitals, businesses, public utilities, State government agencies, offices of the Clerks of Superior Court, and other depositories and holders of money and property. The escheated money is held in trust for the rightful owners.

The primary purpose of the escheat program is to bring these assets under the control of the State for the benefit of the people of North Carolina. The Treasurer invests the escheated monies in the same manner that State retirement and trust funds are invested. Income derived from this fund is distributed annually to the State Education Assistance Authority to be used to make loans to worthy and needy North Carolina resident students enrolled in State public institutions of higher education. In 1993, a total of $7.7 million in loans was made to some 2,350 deserving students.

Unclaimed property. A diligent effort is made to find and notify owners of unclaimed property. The Treasurer's office has been recognized for a number of years as having one of the best programs in the country for locating recipients of unclaimed property. While State law requires only that a list of names and addresses of property owners be mailed to the Clerk of Superior Court in the county in which they last resided, other efforts to find the last known address of rightful owners have been initiated. For example, the Treasurer provides local newspapers, radio and television stations with a list of unclaimed property and the names of owners. In addition, data bases of the Departments of Revenue, Division of Motor Vehicles and commercial credit bureaus are cross-referenced to locate property owners.

In 1992, the 3,319 rightful owners of some $2,150,280 were both surprised and grateful when informed of their forgotten property.

Other Duties

North Carolina's Treasurer serves ex-officio on more boards and commissions than any other State official, including the Governor. The Treasurer is a member of the Council of State; Chairman and presiding officer of the Local Government Commission; Chairman of the Tax Review Board; Chairman of the State Banking Commission; Chairman of the Board of Trustees, Teachers' and State Employees' Retirement System; Chairman, Board of Trustees, Local Governmental Employees' Retirement System; Chairman, Firemen's and Rescue Squad Workers' Pension Fund; member of the State Board of Education; member of the State Board of Community Colleges; member of the Capital Planning Commission; member of the North Carolina Housing Commission, and member of the North Carolina Global TransPark Authority, among others.

The Treasurer sits on these boards and commissions because the General Assembly has realized that the unique knowledge and experience of the State's chief financial officer is a valuable asset to these organizations.

Despite its great responsibility and wide ranging duties, the Department of State Treasurer is one of the smallest departments in State government. In 1993, the Department had 249 employees and a budget of $15.2 million.

Chapter 11

Parting Thoughts For Improving Life In North Carolina

Unquestionably, we must do a better job in the future managing North Carolina's financial resources than we've done in the recent past. Our survival as a free and democratic society is intricately linked to the prudent use of limited resources. Our people are becoming cynical toward government, at all levels, and unless we act to rebuild and maintain the public trust, citizens will become openly disenchanted and will withhold their support. We must change the way government operates and the way we provide its governance.

The public's business is big business and it is a business open for discussion, or it should be. Within the bounds of the Constitution of North Carolina, the role and purpose of State government is determined by the General Assembly–men and women elected to represent the taxpaying public. The General Assembly's adoption of the budget gives meaning to the programs and services to be provided the people of North Carolina. The State budget does two things: it identifies the resources to be collected, in the form of taxes and fees, and it sets the maximum expenditures authorized for the departments and agencies of State government. Under our Constitution, expenditures authorized cannot exceed projected resources.

We face a real dilemma in North Carolina, as in the nation. Public spending has been increasing faster than the ability of our people to pay taxes. It is unfortunate that our government leaders have come to believe there are only two solutions: raise taxes or reduce spending. The fact is, there are other solutions, among them, make government work, make government effective, make government more efficient, make government responsive to the people and privatize some government programs. People have indicated they do not want less education, fewer roads, less health care, unsafe neighborhoods or reductions in many other public services. They want better education, better roads, better health care and other improved services for the same tax dollar.

In the wake of these conflicting demands, a new kind of public institution is required. Public institutions of the future will be lean, decentralized and innovative. They must be flexible, adaptable and quick to learn new ways when conditions change. They respond to competition and customer choice and they are sensitive to other non-bureaucratic mechanisms to get things done quickly, creatively and effectively.

Rowing and Steering

The word government is from the Latin word, "gubanare," which means "to steer." The job of government is to steer. Delivering government services is "rowing." In state and local governments, where budgets have to balance, we have learned that we can steer more effectively if we let others do more of the rowing. Steering is very difficult, however, if an organization's best energies and resources are devoted to rowing.

Governments that focus on steering make more policy decisions. They put more social and economic institutions into motion. Rather than hiring more public employees, they make sure other institutions are delivering services and meeting the community's needs. In contrast, governments preoccupied with service delivery often abdicate this steering function. Public leaders, who get caught on the tax-and-spend treadmill, have to work so hard to keep their service systems together–running faster and faster just to stay in the same place–that they have no time left to think about steering.

The objective of government should be simply to "buy" a defined level of service–defined by quantity and quality. This means that a modern government management system must be mission driven and results oriented. The desired outcome of most services is satisfied customers. Quality is determined by customers, not providers. Few people in government today ever use the word customer and that is one of government's shortcomings.

The people who work in government are not the problem–the systems in which they work are the problem. It is said that only 15 percent of the problems in most organizations are caused by the workers and managers. The other 85 percent of the problems are systemic. In government that means our education system, the budget system, the personnel system, and many other systems are archaic, outmoded, inefficient, and ineffective.

Entrepreneurial governments will abandon old programs and methods. They will be innovative, imaginative and creative. They cannot fear working with the private sector. It is essential they employ good business judgments. They must privatize wherever practical. They must create enterprises and revenue generating operations. They must be market oriented. They will reward merit. They will need knowledgeable, inspired and motivated workers, good research and sound infrastructure.

While governments are not like businesses in every sense of the word, governments can become more entrepreneurial and must do so to rebuild public support. Under intense fiscal pressure, state and local leaders nationwide have no choice but to change the way they do business. The closer a government is to its citizens, the more accountable its officials tend to be and the more likely they are to craft practical solutions, rather than create one-size-fits-all programs.

In North Carolina, we have a history of bold and innovative actions, and we have made good government a habit. Now, we have that marvelous opportunity once again to be above average–to provide innovative, imaginative and affordable government.

In that spirit, here are some closing thoughts relating to specific modifications which ought to be made to State government in North Carolina.

The Past Is Prologue

The history of public finance and the history of North Carolina's growth and prosperity has been inextricably linked to the history of transportation and education. Make no mistake about it–roads make money. But we also must have an educated workforce.

Good government, good schools and good roads–these are the elements which have been central to the thinking of the people of North Carolina. In 1931, the people of this State stood at the crossroads. They faced then the test of governmental survival. The consequences of the Great Depression were staggering. State and local governments were literally broke. Yet, they faced questions: How could they build and operate better public schools? How could they develop and maintain a statewide system of roads? How could they manage the public funds more wisely and in such a manner that government would become the solution to many of the common problems, not another problem in and of itself?

Our forefathers met that challenge then, with courage and honor. They established a system of public finance that today endures as the envy of the nation. But now we are faced with the same challenges that our predecessors faced some six decades ago. Only the magnitude of the problems is different.

The Budget Process

The budget hoop we jump through today in North Carolina State government was devised in 1925—the year the Executive Budget Act was enacted— at a time when most State employees were housed in or near the Capitol building and could be seen and counted, coming to work every morning. It is hard to imagine today, with our State workforce of 217,000 employees, but just 69 years ago, the entire executive branch, judicial branch, including the Supreme Court, and the General Assembly, worked out of the same building.

We should move from a line-item budget, which is staid and inflexible, to a mission-driven budget which is adaptable to changing needs. The ground rules for the adoption and administration of the State budget today have little resemblance to the needs and complexities of the people we serve today.

In the budget process we follow today, a major determining factor is "how much did you spend last year?" Instead, the major concern should be, "What do we need to do today to serve the people?"

It should come as no surprise today that our State government now is too large and inefficient. The budget process we have in place today rewards spending by the process of spending itself. A good manager who spends his budget for only what is needed, is punished by having his budget cut back the next year. A manager who squanders his resources is rewarded by more money next year.

As a beginning step in revisiting this process, the State ought to publish and provide to the people, a concise and full report summarizing all of the programs and services—with their costs identified. Such a document would surprise a lot of people. And it would precipitate a demand for change.

Our first step in creating better government should be to change the system by which we develop and adopt the budget. The only way to meet new needs, expand current, worthwhile programs or continue existing programs with increased costs is to reallocate resources. In doing so, we must make choices.

Taxes

Undoubtedly, our current system of taxation, which is now based on the federal tax structure has serious flaws. It is overly complex. It fosters a large underground economy. It encourages dubious tax shelters. It engenders a perception of unfairness. And, it breeds contempt for government in general. When the average taxpayer equates the tax burden to all levels of government and concludes there is too little effort by government to measure the results of public expenditures and little interest in making sure government programs work efficiently and effectively, this is when the public trust begins to erode.

The value of the tax dollar has two sides. One side is the taxpayer's labor and effort to earn wages and his or her willingness to share a portion of those wages with his or her government. On the other hand are those who benefit from government programs–schools, hospitals, highways, justice and many other essential public services. To do the good things which government needs to do, you must take from taxpayers and give to those who benefit. It should be a fair and equitable process. Neither should dominate. State government must be both sensitive to the taxpayer and responsive to the citizen.

New revenue sources and alternatives may be devised to avoid the necessity to increase taxes. Improved management and better use of resources can provide additional funds to respond to new needs. Taxpayers have made it clear they are opposed to higher taxes, certainly not until serious efforts are made to make government efficient and effective.

Privatization

Privatization, the process of turning over to the private, free-enterprise sector those functions which it can do better than government, is the tide of the future. The best example of how this partnership between government and private enterprise has existed for decades is within the Department of Transportation. There, government managers and technicians design the roads, determine specifications and establish schedules. The General Assembly appropriates money. Private companies bid to do the actual work. The company which can meet the State's requirements at the lowest cost to taxpayers wins the contract.

Through that public/private partnership, North Carolina has built the largest state-maintained highway system in America. Our highways are also among the best in America.

Could we not do the same with our schools? I think so.

Successful governments of the future, which have regained public trust will have explored every possibility for building effective partnerships with the private sector.

The New North Carolina

There is little doubt that our governmental programs in North Carolina, like those of our national government, have become excessively and unnecessarily bloated and bureaucratized. Numerous studies have documented this fact. Instead of correcting the problems, too often, our leaders who had the power to make the changes have chosen instead to put these studies on the shelves, where other similar studies gather dust, and continue with the status quo.

History has taught us that huge, impersonal centralized government is seldom reversible. The nature of entrenched government bureaucracy is that it grows, feeding off of the sweat and toil of the working men and women, and continues to grow as long as the people who pay taxes will tolerate higher taxes.

Government bloat will continue to demand resources long after programs have ceased to be useful. The fundamental function of government is political, and therein lies the problem. To achieve its goals, the governmental bureaucracy will cater to the whims of powerful, special interests in order to achieve its own comfort and security. The taxpayer is the loser because he has to pay for it all.

It comes as no surprise that we are now living in a "new" North Carolina, politically, economically, socially and culturally. Critical aspects of these areas of our life have been in a state of transition for some time. The most profound change, which is affecting how we deal with and manage the other areas of change, is the political revolution that has taken place in North Carolina during the recent past.

North Carolina was governed by one political party from 1900 to 1972. The Democratic Party, though divided by conservatives and progressives within its own ranks, prevailed for nearly three quarters of a century. That has changed. No longer does winning a Democratic primary election mean that election to statewide office is a sure thing. Primaries are still hard-fought but general elections are more even-footed as well. The result is a new balance of power in almost every election. This shift of political power is beginning to influence the State's financial decisions. Even in the General Assembly, long dominated by Democrats, the power is shifting. Women, minorities and Republicans have gained greater influence in the legislature in recent years. In the 1992 election, Republicans won 42 seats in the State House of Representatives and were just 19 votes short of becoming the majority party. That fact alone should guarantee a more responsible approach toward managing the State's resources, especially the public purse.

Too often in recent years our national leaders, and to a lesser extent our State leaders, have stretched the definition of the public purpose to include the expenditure of public funds which benefit only a narrow constituency. That is not good public policy for several reasons. First, it is not consistent with the requirement of our constitution that tax money be spent only for the public purpose. Second, it is not fair—a guiding principle which girds the foundation of our democratic form of government. And finally, when a few special interest groups gain excessive power, through their political clout and use that power in a way that is perceived to be unfair, the people become suspicious and cynical about their government.

We see the evidence of such cynicism about us already. It exists in the growth of the underground economy, in low voter turnout, in letters to the editor, in the rapid growth of radio talk shows and their highly popular government-bashing agenda. And it exists in opinion polls, which have shown for some time that citizens in this State and in this nation have lost respect for many public leaders.

No longer can we fall back into the old ways of life, where a few powerful people dictated State policy. We must instead return the power to the people and conduct the public's business in the open in a way that benefits all citizens fairly. We must never lose sight of the fact that the public purse is what it purports to be. It belongs to the people, not the officeholders who have been entrusted with its safekeeping.

Conclusion

How does one conclude a commentary on the history of public finance in North Carolina? The simple answer is you don't. A new chapter is being written each and every day and every year. In truth, we can only toast our past and remain optimistic about the future. While our State government will always sit at the crosscurrents of challenge and opportunity, and while people with leadership qualities will continue to come and go, the channels will be there awaiting those who will pick up the oars to pursue those waters of opportunity.

A Special Tribute

Many people have played important roles in keeping and safeguarding North Carolina's public purse. I would like to personally recognize and thank each of them who have worked diligently. Several have been especially helpful during my career and I extend a special appreciation to them:

Edwin T. Barnes, 1965-90 - accountant, local government financial consultant, Deputy Secretary of the Local Government Commission, Director of the Retirement System and Deputy State Treasurer. A 25-year veteran of the department, he was professional, dedicated, good with details and analytical.

Thomas H. Campbell, 1990-present - Assistant State Treasurer. He is a quick learner, energetic, easy to work with and eager to take on all assignments—no matter how tough. He has a great future.

C. Douglas Chappell, 1966-present - accounting clerk, administrative assistant, accountant, assistant to State Investment Officer, assistant State Investment Officer, State Investment Officer, Director of Investment and Banking Division and Deputy State Treasurer. He started at the bottom of the ranks and worked his way to the top. He is totally dedicated and North Carolina is fortunate to have his talent, energy and commitment.

Dennis D. Ducker, 1969-present - retirement field representative, supervisor of field services, administrative officer, assistant to the State Treasurer, assistant Director of the Retirement Systems, Director of the Retirement Systems and Deputy State Treasurer. A proven performer, well-read and always on top of the important issues. He has moved upward through the ranks and is a most deserving employee.

Baxter Durham, 1941-45 - executive secretary of the Teachers' and State Employees' Retirement System and Local Governmental Employees' Retirement Systems during the early years of the programs. His diligence helped the program get started on a good foundation. His footprints will always be here.

William E. Easterling, 1932-68 - Secretary of the Local Government Commission. For 36 years he was recognized as a giant in public finance throughout the State. He was the right man at the right time to provide excellent and badly needed leadership to local governments.

John D. Foust, 1976-89 - Secretary of the Local Government Commission, Director of State and Local Government Finance Division and Deputy State Treasurer. His knowledge of the many facets of public finance, his great memory of people and places served the program well. He was an excellent negotiator and mediator, beloved by everyone who knew him.

William H. Hambleton, 1958-78 - accountant, chief accountant, assistant Director of the Retirement Systems, Director of the Retirement Systems and Deputy State Treasurer. An easy going, highly capable and professional person who grew up with the program and helped make it into one of the nation's best.

Robert M. High, 1982-present - accounting manager, Secretary of the Local Government Commission, Director of State and Local Government Finance Division and Deputy State Treasurer. Highly trained and possesses great insight into current issues. Loves details and knows accounting theory.

J. Everett Miller, 1968-73 - Director of the Retirement Systems.

Christopher S. Moore, 1976-82 - State Investment Officer, Director of the Investment and Banking Division and Deputy State Treasurer.

James C. Moore, 1956-present - accounting clerk, administrative assistant, administrative officer, operations officer, Director of Administrative Services Division and Deputy State Treasurer. Always ready and willing and is the perfect example of the adage that "experience in the best teacher." A man of few words, he has been a tremendous asset to the department.

R. Ray Moore, 1934-76 - cashier, principal cashier, State Investment Officer and assistant State Treasurer. Knew State government inside and out. Commanded great respect among Wall Street professionals. His contribution to the investment program will be everlasting.

Linville B. Parker, 1921-59 - clerk, Chief Administrative Officer and Deputy State Treasurer. An easy-going leader and a good teacher.

Thomas C. Wagstaff, 1978-88 - Assistant to the Treasurer. A walking encyclopedia, philosophical and wise, and the department's resident counselor and advisor.

Nathan Yelton, 1945-68 - executive secretary of Teachers' and State Employees' Retirement Systems and Local Governmental Employees' Retirement System. A good problem solver.

Faye M. Smith, 1963-present, and **Shirley P. Stell**, 1973-present - executive assistants to the State Treasurer. Their loyalty, great competence, and total commitment has been a major contribution to the department. Without their unselfish dedication, we would not have been able to do our jobs.

Bibliography

Ashe, Samuel A., Stephen B.Weeks, and Charles L. Van Noppen, eds. *Biographical History of North Carolina, From Colonial Times to Present.* 8 vols. Greensboro: Charles. L. Van Noppen, Publisher, 1905-1917.

Boyd, William K. *History of North Carolina.* Vol. II, *The Federal Period 1783-1860.* Chicago and New York: The Lewis Publishing Company, 1919.

Bye, Raymond T. *Principles of Economics.* New York: F. S. Crofts & Company, 1924.

Cross, Jerry L. "Biographical Sketches of Seven State Treasurers." North Carolina Department of Cultural Resources, Raleigh, North Carolina, 1994.

Department of the State Treasurer. *An Accountability Report and A New Highway Financing Plan for North Carolina, The Good Roads State.* Raleigh, North Carolina, 1993.

Department of the State Treasurer. *Treasurers' Reports, 1830-1994.* Raleigh, North Carolina.

Hamilton, J. G. de Roulhoc, ed. *Papers of William A. Graham.* Raleigh: State Archives and History, 1957.

Lefler, Hugh Talmage, and Albert Ray Newsome. *The History of A Southern State, North Carolina.* Chapel Hill: University of North Carolina Press, 1963.

Liner, Charles D., "The Origins and Development of the North Carolina System of Taxation." *Popular Government* 45 (Summer 1979): 41-49.

Lipsey, Richard G., Peter O. Steiner, and Douglas D. Purvis. *Economics.* 8th ed. New York: Harper & Row, 1987.

Macon, Hershal L. "A Fiscal History of North Carolina 1776-1860." Ph.D. diss., University of North Carolina, Chapel Hill, 1932.

Morgan, Kathleen O'Leary, Scott Morgan, and Neal Quitno, eds. *State Rankings 1992, A Statistical View of the 50 United States.* Lawrence, Kansas: Morgan Quitno Corporation, 1992.

North Carolina Department of Agriculture. *1993 Agricultural Statistics.* Raleigh, North Carolina, 1994.

North Carolina Department of Tax Research. *Historical Background of the North Carolina Income Tax.* Raleigh, North Carolina, 1956.

North Carolina General Assembly, 1993 Session. Fiscal Research Division of the North Carolina General Assembly. *Overview, Fiscal and Budgetary Actions.* Raleigh, North Carolina, 1993.

Office of State Budget and Management. *The North Carolina State Budget 1993-95.* Raleigh, North Carolina, 1993.

Osborne, David and Ted Gaebler. *Reinventing Government: How the Entrepreneurial Spirit is Transforming the Public Sector.* Reading, Massachusetts: Addison-Wesley Publishing Company, 1992.

Powell, William S. *Dictionary of North Carolina Biography.* 5 vols. Chapel Hill: University of North Carolina Press, 1979-1994.

State Data Center, Office of State Budget and Management. *Statistical Abstract of North Carolina Counties, 1991.* Raleigh, North Carolina, 1991.

Webber, Carolyn, and Aaran Wildavsky. *A History of Taxation and Expenditure in the Western World.* New York: Simon and Schuster, 1986.

Wheeler, John W. *Historical Sketches of North Carolina from 1584 to 1851.* Philadelphia: Lippincott, Grambo and Company, 1851.

Appendix I

North Carolina Budget, Fiscal Year 1800

Cash Balance as of Nov. 1, 1800	$135,358
Revenue	
Taxation	$38,000
Land Sales	5,800
Total	$43,800
Expenditures	
General Assembly	$30,000
Executive Branch	8,000
Judicial Branch	9,000
Miscellaneous	1,000
Total	$48,000

Source: Hershal L. Macon, "A Fiscal History of North Carolina 1776-1860" (Ph.D. diss., University of North Carolina, Chapel Hill, 1932). [Note: Compiled from the N.C. Senate and House Journals on the basis of Reports of the Treasurer, pp. 52-70.]

Appendix II

North Carolina Budget, Fiscal Year 1900

Cash Balance as of Nov. 1, 1898	$190,175
Revenue	
Public Taxes	320,000
Business Taxes	50,000
Other Sources	50,000
Licenses	30,000
Total	$450,000
Expenditures	
General Assembly	$65,000
Interest on State Debt	65,000
Executive Branch	13,500
Judicial Branch	33,500
Pensions	60,000
Higher Education	34,000
Penitentiary	20,500
Railroad Commission	5,250
State Guard	3,000
State Hospitals	140,000
Miscellaneous	10,250
Total	$450,000

State Debt: $6,331,770
Source: Report of the Treasurer, 1990.

Appendix III

Projected North Carolina Budget, Fiscal Year 2000

Projected Cash Balance July 1, 2000
$200 million

Revenue	
Individual Income Tax	$6.20 billion
Sales Tax	3.80 billion
Corporate Income Tax	.70 billion
Nontax Revenue	.40 billion
Other Taxes	1.60 billion
Highway Taxes & Fees	1.60 billion
Federal Government	5.80 billion
Other	1.90 billion
Total	$22.00 billion
Expenditures	
General Assembly	.03 billion
Education	8.20 billion
Human Resources	7.80 billion
Justice	1.70 billion
Highways	2.20 billion
General Government	.50 billion
Environment/Health	.60 billion
Debt Service	.20 billion
Capital Improvements	.40 billion
Miscellaneous	.34 billion
Total	$22.00 billion

Appendix IV

North Carolina State Population, Income, Consumer Price Index and Budget for Selected Years, 1960-1992

Year	Population	Total Income	Real Per Capita Income	CPI	Total State Budget
1960	4,573,000	7.4 billion	$5,483	29.6	.6 billion
1970	5,099,000	16.4 billion	8,332	38.8	1.7 billion
1980	5,898,000	47.1 billion	9,709	82.4	5.4 billion
1990	6,653,000	108.9 billion	12,529	130.7	12.9 billion
1992	6,843,000	123.1 billion	12,820	140.3	14.5 billion

Sources: North Carolina population and total personal income, U.S. Department of Commerce, Bureau of Economic Analysis; consumer price index for all urban consumers 1982-84 = 100, U.S. Department of Labor, Bureau of Labor Statistics; state budget, *1993 Legislative Overview*, Appendix 4.

Appendix V

History of North Carolina Sales Tax

1933	Enacted at 3 percent rate, with maximum tax of $10 per single article.
1935	Limited use tax levied on motor vehicles at same rates as the sales tax.
1937	Maximum tax per article increased to $15.
1955	Maximum tax per article repealed.
1991	Sales tax increased to 4 percent

A preferential rate of 1 percent is given to the buyers of farm and manufacturing machinery, newspaper presses, broadcast equipment, central office equipment and communications equipment. In addition, a maximum tax of $80 per purchase is charged for these special items. In 1989, motor vehicles became subject to a highway use tax of 3 percent with a minimum tax of $40 and a maximum tax of $1,000 per single vehicle. Aircraft, boats and railway cars are subject to a 2 percent tax with a $1,500 maximum.

Note: In addition to the State sales tax, counties may levy and collect an additional 2 percent on general consumer purchases. In addition, some counties have obtained special permission to collect additional hotel occupancy and restaurant taxes.

Appendix VI

Sales and Use Tax Collections, Fiscal Year 1992-93

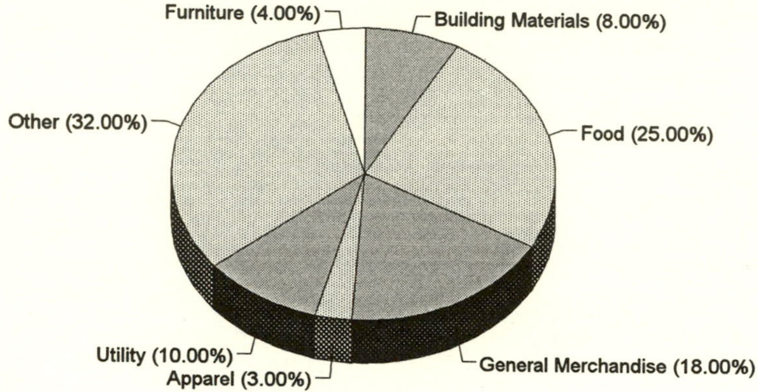

Appendix VII

Total State Budget By Source Of Funds
(In Millions)

Fiscal Year	General Fund*	Federal Revenue Sharing	Highway Fund	Federal	Other	Total
1974-75	$1,734.6	$57.2	$ 392.7	$ 648.6	$ 247.8	$ 3,080.9
1975-76	1,733.2	51.7	422.8	747.6	292.3	3,247.6
1976-77	1,922.4	67.1	414.6	776.8	282.9	3,463.8
1977-78	2,158.0	66.9	433.1	967.9	351.4	3,977.3
1978-79	2,515.4	62.5	461.8	1,042.7	328.5	4,410.9
1979-80	2,787.7	57.0	497.6	1,240.5	448.8	5,031.7
1980-81	3,216.4	28.4	506.1	1,296.5	395.7	5,443.1
1981-82	3,435.0	0.0	535.0	1,312.7	470.0	5,752.8
1982-83	3,623.6	0.0	555.6	1,322.3	485.9	5,987.4
1983-84	3,876.6	0.0	664.0	1,597.4	584.9	6,718.9
1984-85	4,516.6	0.0	713.6	1,655.8	551.7	7,437.7
1985-86	5,130.6	0.0	735.5	1,838.1	696.4	8,400.6
1986-87	5,531.4	0.0	839.4	1,887.4	698.3	8,956.5
1987-88	5,977.9	0.0	882.4	2,026.8	837.1	9,724.2
1988-89	6,586.1	0.0	918.7	2,117.4	788.2	10,410.4
1989-90	7,360.0	0.0	1,236.6	2,366.8	1,033.0	11,996.4
1990-91	8,149.6*	0.0	1,223.8	2,616.8	949.4	12,939.6
1991-92	7,983.0*	0.0	1,323.3	3,127.8	1,176.3	13,610.4
1992-93	8,209.5	0.0	1,318.4	3,617.6	1,363.2	14,508.7
1993-94	9,378.6	0.0	1,363.3	4,516.4	1,456.5	16,714.8

Source: Post Legislative Budget Summary 1993-95, 308.
*Includes Legislative Bonds for Capital Improvements

Appendix VIII

Highway Trust Fund Revenue, Fiscal Year 1993-94

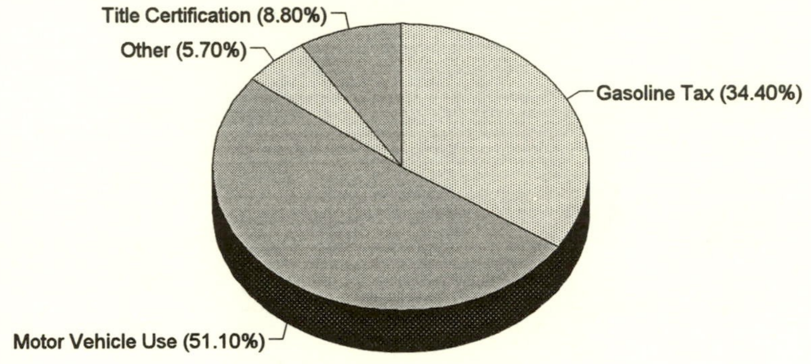

Appendix IX

Trends in General Fund Operating Budget

(in millions)

Fiscal Year	Public Education	Higher Education	Community Colleges	Human Resources	Correction	General Government	Total
1974-75	$ 789.4	$ 280.6	$109.2	$ 270.4	$ 71.0	$ 177.8	$1,698.4
1975-76	800.9	270.5	105.5	282.5	68.7	209.6	1,737.7
1976-77	899.2	307.1	116.5	335.8	73.8	230.6	1,963.0
1977-78	997.7	357.8	114.1	368.2	92.9	262.7	2,193.4
1978-79	1,098.2	394.8	139.8	412.6	103.5	303.1	2,452.0
1979-80	1,230.1	436.9	145.2	473.7	120.3	344.8	2,751.0
1980-81	1,390.9	515.3	174.9	532.8	141.6	395.5	3,151.0
1981-82	1,495.3	567.6	194.5	562.5	158.4	423.4	3,401.7
1982-83	1,515.8	599.2	205.6	589.5	171.6	479.4	3,561.1
1983-84	1,619.0	641.5	232.2	615.6	186.5	477.2	3,772.0
1984-85	1,886.7	747.0	259.1	676.6	208.6	541.6	4,319.6
1985-86	2,185.8	840.3	281.9	747.6	231.0	590.5	4,877.1
1986-87	2,346.1	909.1	307.1	804.9	248.2	618.3	5,233.7
1987-88	2,639.2	980.7	326.3	874.4	274.2	710.4	5,805.2
1988-89	2,930.6	1,039.5	332.1	961.2	311.4	727.6	6,302.4
1989-90	3,134.4	1,118.0	365.9	1,012.3	376.7	875.7	6,883.0
1990-91	3,329.2	1,143.0	387.6	1,100.0	428.0	861.8	7,249.6
1991-92	3,291.4	1,121.1	344.1	1,239.4	475.5	879.0	7,350.5
1992-93	3,434.0	1,173.9	398.4	1,401.9	508.4	960.9	7,877.5
1993-94	3,628.7	1,227.8	423.6	1,716.6	558.7	1,118.7	8,674.1

Note: 1989-90 actions of the General Assembly authorized a new Department of Environment, Health and Natural Resources. The change of $82.5 million from the Department of Human Resources to the new Department is included under General Government.

Appendix X

Trends in Population Served: State Education Programs, 1974-75 to 1993-94

Fiscal Year	Public Education ADM[a]	% Change	Higher Education FTE[b]	% Change	Community Colleges FTE[b]	% Change
1974-75	1,160,363	0.6%	86,678	7.2%	94,409	34.1%
1975-76	1,167,014	0.6%	92,253	6.0%	102,451	7.8%
1976-77	1,183,191	1.4%	92,224	0.0%	97,592	-5.0%
1977-78	1,174,302	-0.8%	94,248	2.1%	104,948	7.0%
1978-79	1,155,501	-1.6%	95,375	1.2%	115,631	9.2%
1979-80	1,142,552	-1.1%	98,012	2.7%	123,645	6.5%
1980-81	1,123,840	-1.7%	101,266	3.2%	129,071	4.2%
1981-82	1,102,951	-1.9%	102,540	1.2%	131,893	2.1%
1982-83	1,092,930	-0.9%	104,098	1.5%	133,767	1.4%
1983-84	1,084,728	-0.8%	104,616	0.5%	130,093	-2.8%
1984-85	1,078,700	-0.6%	105,188	0.5%	127,129	-2.3%
1985-86	1,075,289	-0.3%	107,369	2.0%	137,436	7.5%
1986-87	1,073,524	-0.2%	110,764	3.1%	132,778	-3.5%
1987-88	1,072,934	-0.1%	112,861	1.9%	122,777	-8.1%
1988-89	1,068,800	-0.4%	116,788	3.4%	120,579	-1.8%
1989-90	1,065,399	-0.3%	120,354	3.0%	126,503	4.7%
1990-91	1,070,297	0.5%	123,328	2.4%	134,107	5.7%
1991-92	1,086,380	1.5%	126,139	2.2%	142,936	6.2%
1992-93	1,093,683	0.7%	128,667	2.0%	142,216	-0.5%
1993-94	*1,125,028	2.8%	*131,545	2.2%	*145,022	1.9%

[a]Final Average Daily Membership-database for Budgeted ADM changed in 1986-87 from the projected best three of the first four months ADM to the highest of prior year actual ADM or the projected best three of four months ADM.

[b]Full-time Enrollment

*Budgeted

Appendix XI

Trends in Population Served: Medicaid and AFDC, 1974-75 to 1993-94

Fiscal Year	Medicaid[a]	Percent Change	AFDC[b]	Percent Change
1974-75	-	-	245,465	11.8%
1975-76	-	-	275,775	12.3%
1976-77	-	-	285,988	3.7%
1977-78	455,774	-	279,523	-2.3%
1978-79	453,174	-0.6%	280,171	0.2%
1979-80	455,702	0.6%	280,209	0.0%
1980-81	459,364	0.8%	289,622	3.4%
1981-82	425,233	-7.4%	260,095	-10.2%
1982-83	415,552	-2.3%	258,516	-0.6%
1983-84	407,806	-1.9%	259,093	0.2%
1984-85	414,353	1.6%	215,503	-16.8%
1985-86	441,930	6.7%	222,076	3.1%
1986-87	452,025	2.3%	212,695	-4.2%
1987-88	481,326	6.5%	244,737	15.1%
1988-89	561,053	16.6%	268,760	9.8%
1989-90	638,340	13.8%	290,588	8.1%
1990-91	751,617	17.7%	353,245	21.6%
1991-92	875,968	16.5%	389,847	10.4%
1992-93	986,864	12.7%	419,974	7.7%
1993-94*	1,029,000	4.3%	419,215	-0.2%

[a]Aid to Families with Dependent Children (unduplicated total of recipients).
[b]Number represents actual unduplicated Medicaid eligibles for 1977-78 through 1988-89. Figures prior to 1977-78 are only available in terms of "average monthly" and are not as accurate.

*Estimate

Appendix XII

Trends in Population Served: Corrections Programs, 1974-75 to 1993-94

Fiscal Year	Prison Inmates	Percent Change	Probationers	Percent Change	Parolees	Percent Change
1974-75	11,475	6.6%	31,241	20.8%	5,131	3.1%
1975-76	12,699	10.7%	34,527	10.5%	5,937	15.7%
1976-77	14,359	13.1%	35,412	2.6%	5,948	0.2%
1977-78	14,246	-0.8%	34,692	-2.0%	5,557	-6.6%
1978-79	14,191	-0.4%	34,299	-1.1%	6,824	22.8%
1979-80	15,156	6.8%	36,286	5.8%	4,718	-30.9%
1980-81	16,190	6.8%	39,382	8.5%	5,104	8.2%
1981-82	16,680	3.0%	40,041	1.7%	6,568	28.7%
1982-83	16,500	-1.1%	44,719	11.7%	6,576	0.1%
1983-84	16,583	0.5%	50,111	12.1%	4,345	-33.9%
1984-85	17,181	3.6%	56,380	12.5%	3,909	-10.0%
1985-86	17,741	3.3%	57,982	2.8%	3,520	-10.0%
1986-87	17,112	-3.5%	62,536	7.9%	4,120	17.0%
1987-88	17,468	2.1%	66,949	7.1%	5,500	33.5%
1988-89	17,529	0.3%	71,956	7.5%	6,986	27.0%
1989-90	18,317	4.5%	77,118	7.2%	8,152	16.7%
1990-91	18,911	3.2%	83,219	7.9%	10,087	23.7%
1991-92	19,863	5.0%	87,520	5.2%	12,974	28.6%
1992-93	**21,275	7.1%	*88,613	1.2%	*15,188	17.1%
1993-94	**21,070	-1.0%	*91,271	3.0%	*18,266	20.3%

Note: For consistency in presentation all years have been changed to reflect population or caseload at June 30 of the respective fiscal year.

*Projected
**This may change based on cap revisions.

Appendix XIII

North Carolina State Employees for Selected Years, 1965-1993

Departments	1965	1970	1975	1980	1985	1990	1993
Gen. Government	30,160	39,985	52,452	57,201	57,929	64,756	66,312
Higher Education	15,174	19,367	24,433	25,638	28,229	28,225	32,024
Public Schools	61,121	65,561	74,880	89,886	93,459	107,077	108,649
Comm. Colleges	1,132	3,889	6,872	8,216	8,721	10,005	10,892
Total	107,587	128,802	158,637	180,941	188,338	210,063	217,877

Source: N.C. Office of State Budget and Management.

Note: As of June 30 for each year.

Appendix XIV

Trends In The Number of Teachers and State Employees, 1974-75 to 1993-94

Fiscal Year	Public Education Total	Teachers	Higher Education	Community Colleges	Human Resources
1974-75	73,667	49,969	23,386	5,953	14,921
1975-76	74,880	49,640	24,433	6,872	17,097
1976-77	75,680	49,590	24,215	7,281	17,523
1977-78	81,968	49,692	25,300	6,867	17,724
1978-79	85,892	49,369	25,744	8,102	18,351
1979-80	86,726	48,837	25,387	7,363	18,582
1980-81	89,886	49,322	25,638	8,216	18,585
1981-82	88,978	48,615	25,884	8,438	18,166
1982-83	88,241	47,984	26,354	8,716	17,193
1983-84	88,366	47,631	26,968	8,912	17,665
1984-85	90,123	48,340	27,565	8,866	17,768
1985-86	93,459	50,763	28,229	8,721	17,899
1986-87	94,973	51,127	28,687	9,934	17,766
1987-88	98,333	52,477	29,304	9,945	17,922
1988-89	103,223	55,847	29,866	9,251	17,935
1989-90	105,244	56,593	30,478	9,627	16,823
1990-91	107,077	57,906	28,225	10,005	17,155
1991-92	106,847	59,856	28,702	10,076	17,008
1992-93	108,539	61,148	31,621	10,660	17,159
1993-94	108,649	61,386	32,024	10,892	17,286

Appendix XIV (continued)

Fiscal Year	Correction	Judicial	Transportation	All Other	Total
1974-75	5,191	2,618	15,214	10,750	151,700
1975-76	4,822	2,789	15,431	12,313	158,637
1976-77	4,844	2,937	15,356	11,951	159,787
1977-78	5,804	3,075	15,277	12,061	168,076
1978-79	6,122	3,191	15,382	12,402	175,186
1979-80	6,764	3,396	15,400	12,880	176,498
1980-81	6,804	3,438	15,129	13,245	180,941
1981-82	6,778	3,502	14,689	13,198	179,633
1982-83	7,510	3,508	14,105	12,793	179,140
1983-84	7,750	3,522	14,095	12,742	180,020
1984-85	7,861	3,670	14,546	13,191	183,590
1985-86	7,936	3,755	14,898	13,441	188,338
1986-87	8,191	3,885	14,659	13,588	191,683
1987-88	8,243	3,880	14,712	14,778	197,117
1988-89	9,788	4,047	14,762	13,845	202,717
1989-90	11,209	4,272	14,560	15,468	207,681
1990-91	12,426	4,474	15,044	15,657	210,063
1991-92	13,176	4,471	15,096	15,267	210,643
1992-93	13,336	4,628	15,554	15,427	216,924
1993-94	13,159	4,866	15,370	15,631	217,877